Oshawa Ontario Book 1 in Colour Photos, Saving Our History One Photo at a Time

Photography
by Barbara Raué
©2018

Series Name: Cruising Ontario

Book 204: Oshawa Book 1

Cover photo: 52 Simcoe Street South, Page 22

©All the photos in this book have been taken with my cameras. I own the rights to them.

Series Name: Cruising Ontario
Saving Our History One Photo at a Time
in colour photos

Books Available in Alphabetical Order:
Aberfoyle, Acton, Ajax, Alton, Amherstburg, Ancaster, Arthur, Auburn, Aylmer, Ayr, Beaver Valley, Belgrave, Belleville, Bloomingdale, Blyth, Brantford, Brockville, Burford, Burlington, Caledon, Caledonia, Cambridge, Carlow, Chatsworth, Clifford, Collingwood, Conestogo, Delhi, Dorchester to Aylmer, Drayton, Drumbo, Dundas, Dunlop, Eden Mills, Elmira, Elora, Erin, Essex, Fergus, Goderich, Grimsby, Guelph, Hagersville, Hamilton, Hanover, Harriston, Hespeler, Jarvis, Kingston, Kingsville, Kitchener, Lake Superior, Lincoln, Linwood, Listowel, London, Lucknow, Merrickville, Mono, Mount Forest, Mount Pleasant, Neustadt, New Hamburg, Newboro, Newport, Niagara-on-the-Lake, Oakville, Onondaga, Orangeville, Orillia, Oshawa, Owen Sound, Palmerston, Paris, Pelham, Perth, Peterborough, Petrolia, Pickering, Port Colborne, Port Elgin, Portland, Preston, Rockwood, Sarnia, Sault Ste. Marie, Seaforth, Sheffield, Shelburne, Simcoe, Smiths Falls, Smithville, Southampton, St. Catharines, St. George, St. Jacobs, St. Marys, St. Thomas, Stoney Creek, Stratford, Thamesford, Thunder Bay, Tillsonburg, Toronto, Waterdown, Waterford, Waterloo, Welland, Wellesley, West Flamborough, Westport, Whitby, Windsor, Wingham, Woodstock

Book 200: West Flamborough
Book 201-202: Whitby
Book 203: Ajax and Pickering
Book 204-206: Oshawa

Table of Contents

Fairbanks Street	Page 6
Quebec Street	Page 9
Court Street	Page 11
Olive Avenue	Page 12
Albert Street	Page 12
Simcoe Street South	Page 13
Lloyd Street	Page 24
Oxford Street	Page 27
Cubert Street	Page 28
Mill Street	Page 30
Avenue Street	Page 31
Howard Street	Page 32
Centre Street South	Page 33
Monck Street	Page 39
McGrigor Street	Page 41
Celina Street	Page 46
Athol Street West	Page 46
King Street West	Page 47
King Street East	Page 51
Victoria Street	Page 52
Bond Street East	Page 53
Ontario Street	Page 55

Oshawa is a city in Southern Ontario on the Lake Ontario shoreline. It is about sixty kilometres east of Downtown Toronto. The name Oshawa comes from the Ojibwa word meaning "the crossing place" or "where we must leave our canoes". More than 5,000 people work and more than 2,400 university students study in the downtown core.

Oshawa's roots are tied to the automobile industry with the Canadian division of General Motors located here. It was founded in 1876 as the McLaughlin Carriage Company. The lavish home of the carriage company's founder, Parkwood Estate, is a National Historic Site of Canada.

Historians believe that Oshawa began as a transfer point for the fur trade. Beaver and other animals trapped for their pelts by local natives were traded with the Coureurs des bois (voyagers). Furs were loaded onto canoes by the Mississauga Indians at the Oshawa harbor and transported to the trading posts located to the west at the mouth of the Credit River. Around 1760, the French constructed a trading post near the harbor location; this was abandoned after a few years, but its ruins provided shelter for the first residents of what later became Oshawa.

In the late eighteenth century a local resident, Roger Conant, started an export business shipping salmon to the United States. His success attracted further migration into the region. A large number of the founding immigrants were United Empire Loyalists, who left the United States to live under British rule. Later Irish and then French Canadian immigration increased as did industrialization. Oshawa and the surrounding Ontario County were the settling grounds of a large number of nineteenth century Cornish immigrants. The surveys ordered by Governor John Graves Simcoe, and subsequent land grants, helped populate the area. When Col. Asa Danforth laid out his York-to-Kingston road, it passed through the Oshawa area.

In 1822, a "colonization road" (a north-south road to facilitate settlement) known as Simcoe Street was constructed. It ran from the harbor to the area of Lake Scugog. It intersected the "Kingston Road: at what became Oshawa's "Four Corners."

In 1846 there were about 1,000 people in a community surrounded by farms. There were three churches, a post office, and tradesmen of various types, a foundry, a grist mill and a fulling mill, a brewery, two distilleries, a machine shop and four cabinet makers.

The newly established village became an industrial center, and implement works, tanneries, asheries and wagon factories opened. In 1876, Robert Samuel McLaughlin, Sr. moved his carriage works to Oshawa from Enniskillen to take advantage of its harbor and of the availability of a rail link not too far away. He constructed a two-storey building, which was soon added to. This building was heavily remodeled in 1929, receiving a new facade and being extended to the north. Around 1890, the carriage works relocated from its Simcoe Street address to an unused furniture factory a couple of blocks to the northeast, and this remained its site until the building burnt in 1899. Offered assistance by the town, McLaughlin chose to stay in Oshawa, building a new factory across Mary Street from the old site. Rail service had been provided in 1890 by the Oshawa Railway; this was originally set up as a streetcar line, but by about 1910 a second freight line was built slightly to the east of Simcoe Street which provided streetcar and freight service, connected central Oshawa with the Grand Trunk (now Canadian National) Railway, and with the Canadian Northern (which ran through the very north of Oshawa) and the Canadian Pacific, built in 1912-13.

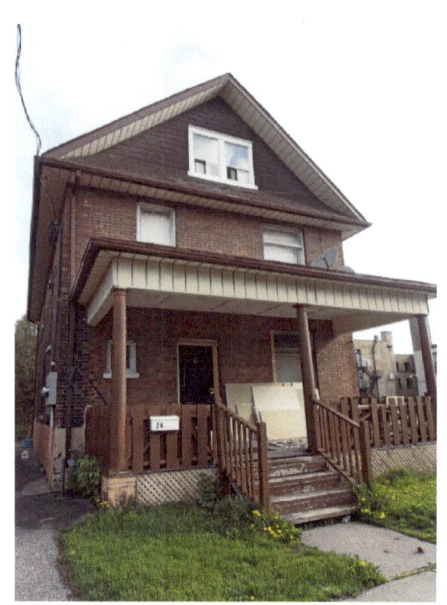

24 Fairbanks Street - Edwardian

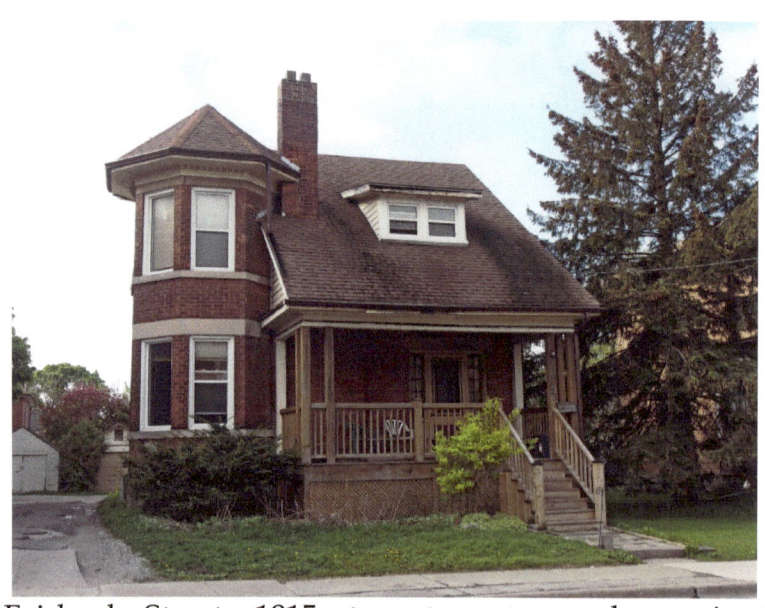

25 Fairbanks Street – 1915 – two-storey tower, dormer in attic

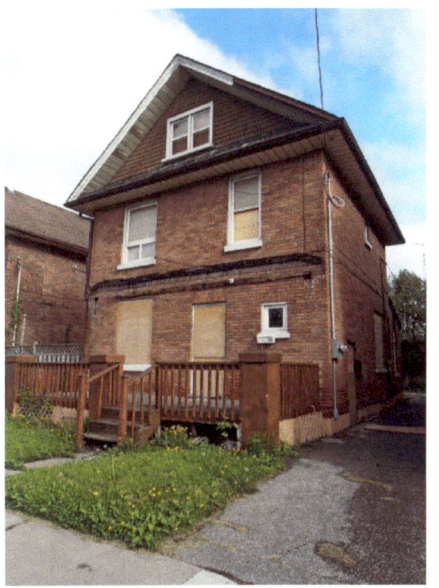 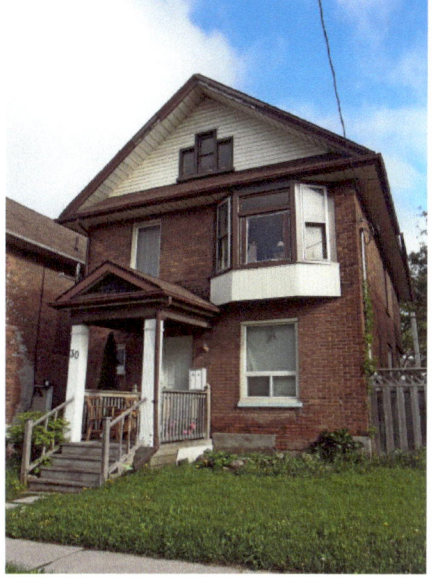

26 Fairbanks Street   30 Fairbanks Street
Edwardian style

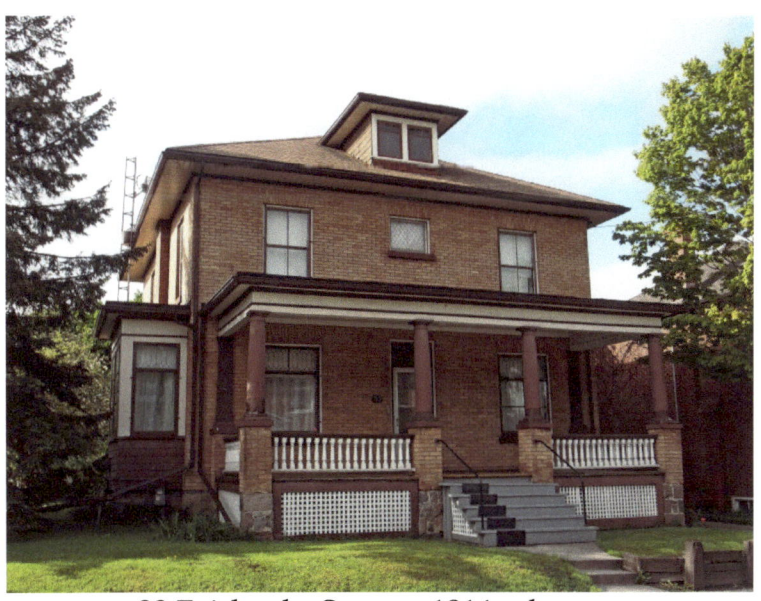

33 Fairbanks Street – 1914 - dormer

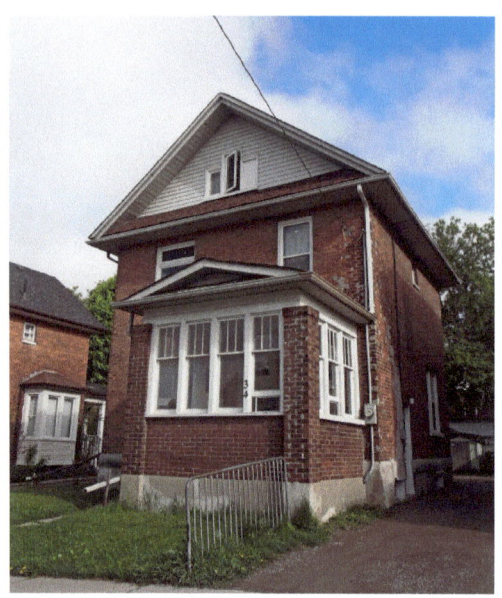

34 Fairbanks Street - Edwardian

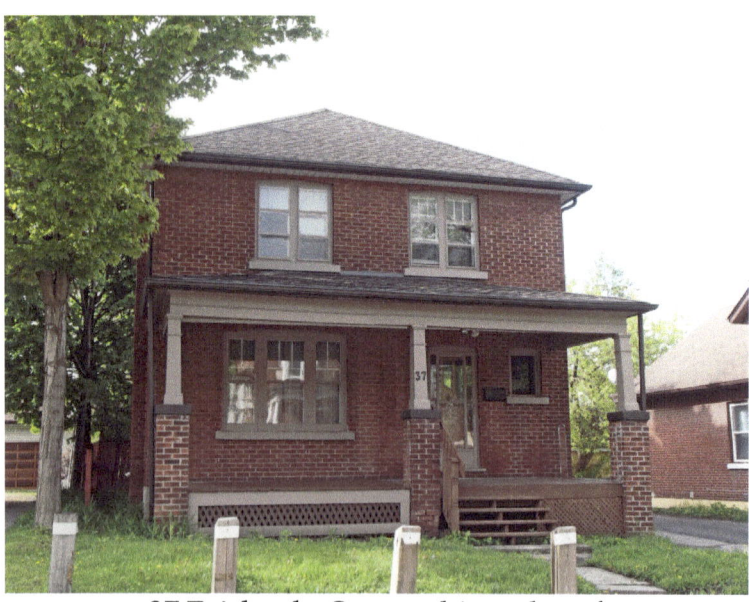

37 Fairbanks Street – hipped roof

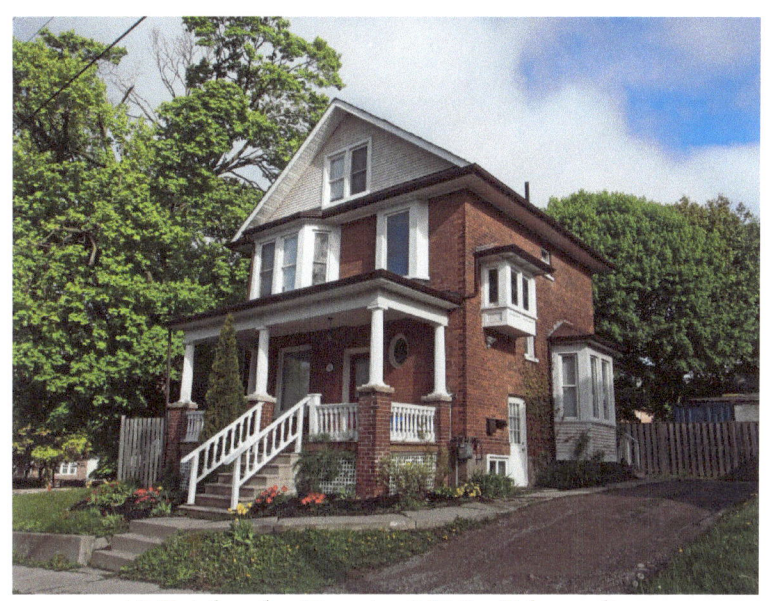

40 Fairbanks Street – 1910 - Edwardian

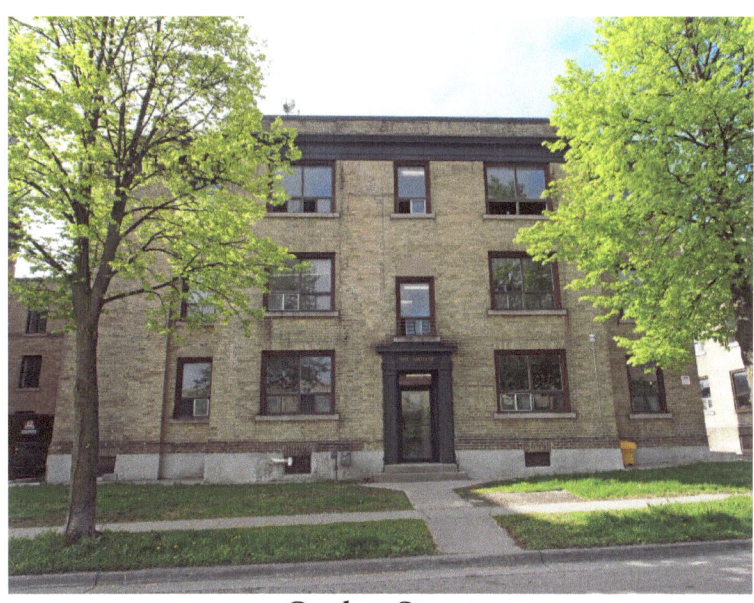

Quebec Street

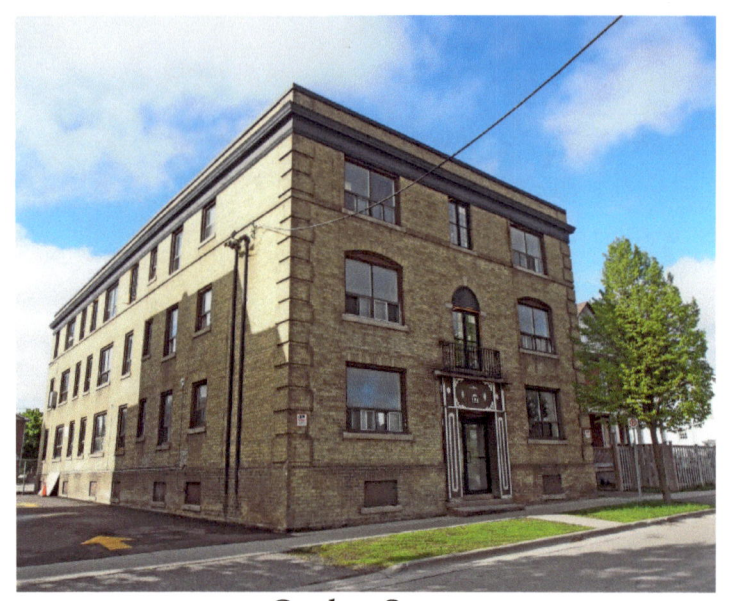

Quebec Street

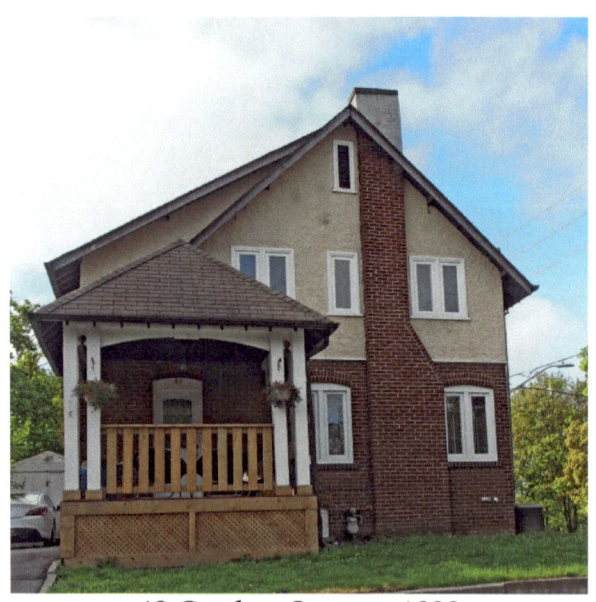

49 Quebec Street – 1922

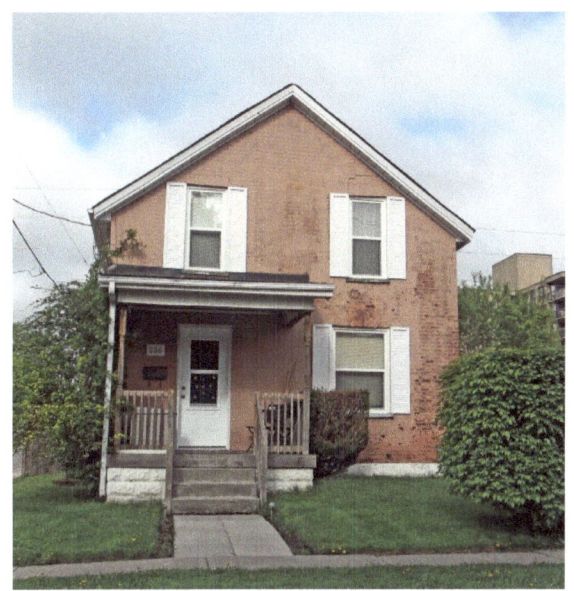

256 Court Street – 1905

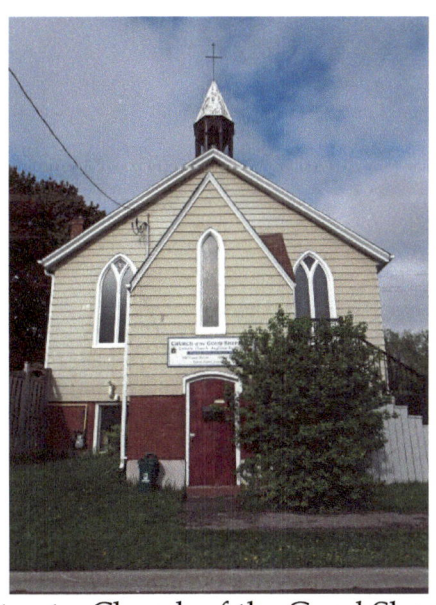

300 Court Street – Church of the Good Shepherd – 1925
Catholic Church – Anglican Tradition

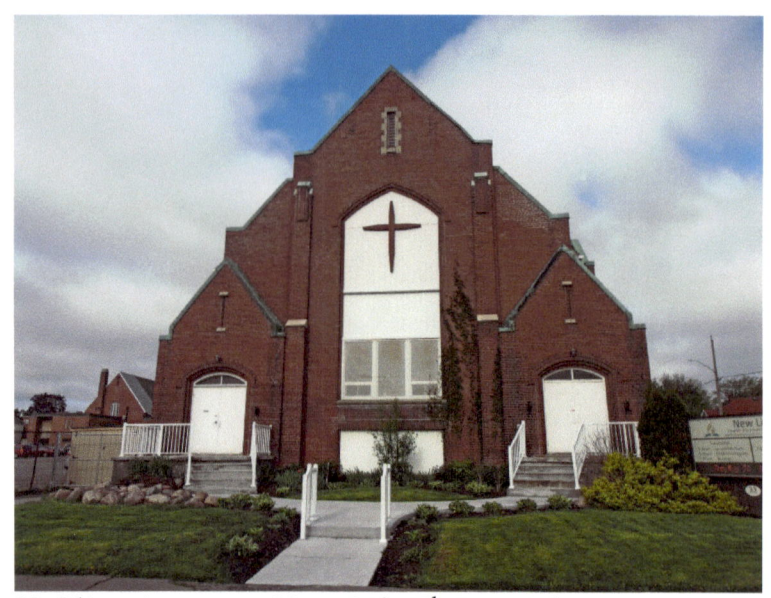

33 Olive Avenue – New Life 7th Day Adventist Church
(former Albert Street United Church) – 1928
– Architect C.C. Stenhouse

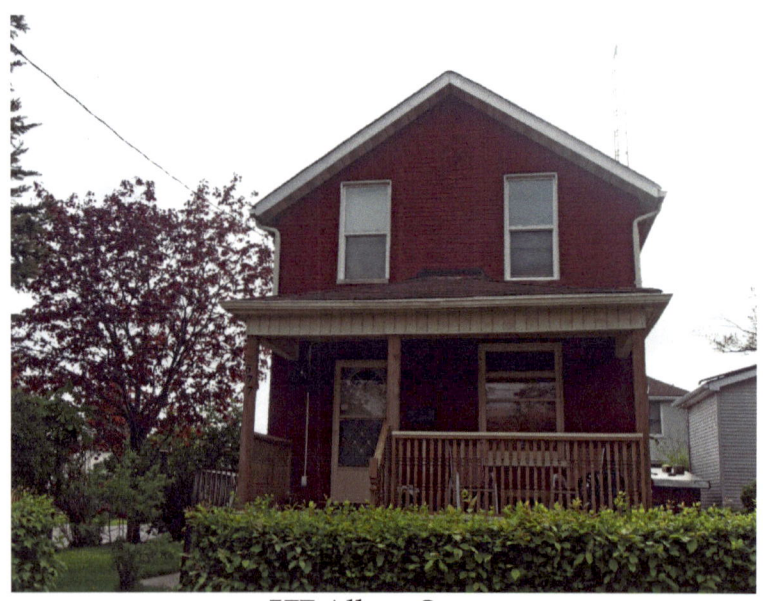

577 Albert Street

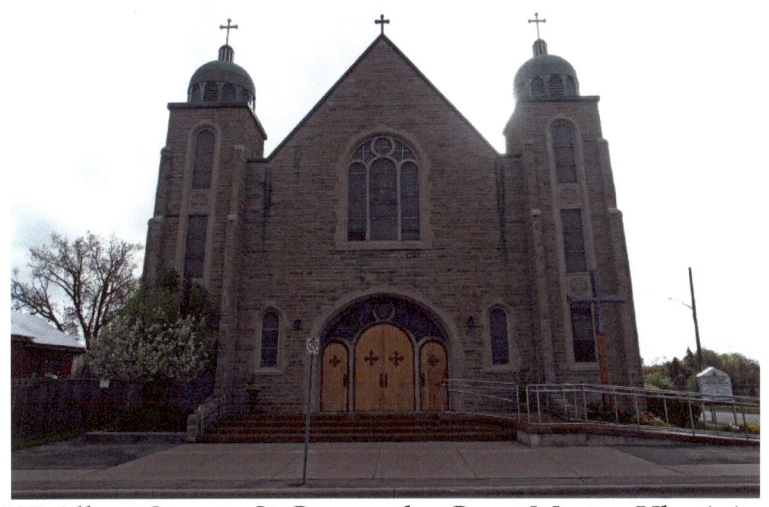

597 Albert Street - St George the Great Martyr Ukrainian Catholic Church – 1955

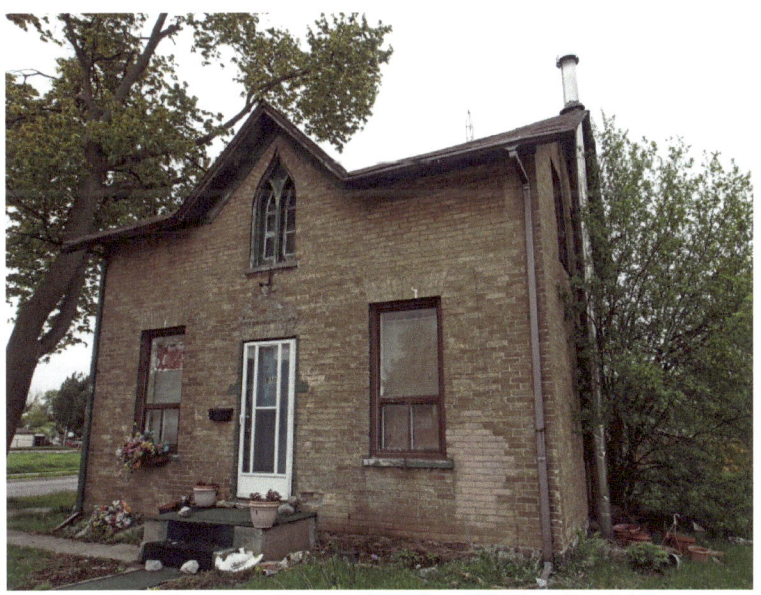

856 Simcoe Street South – 1870 - Gothic

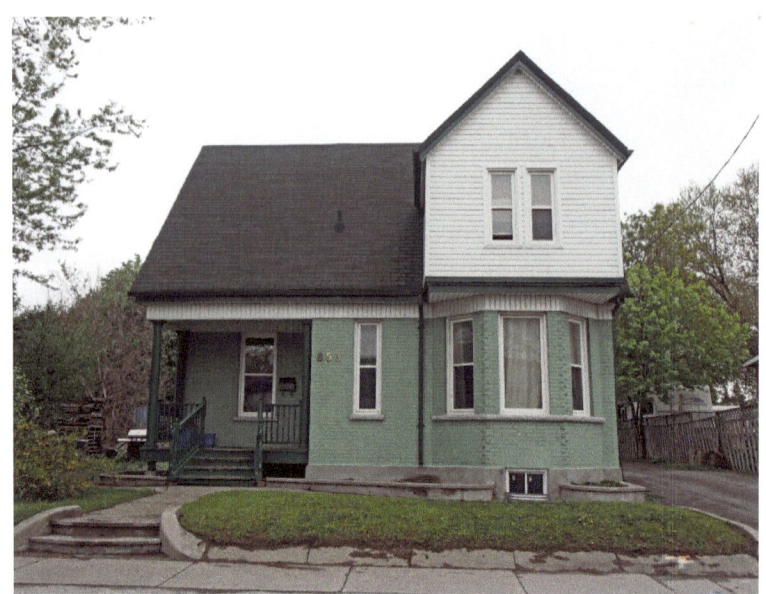
853 Simcoe Street South - 1900

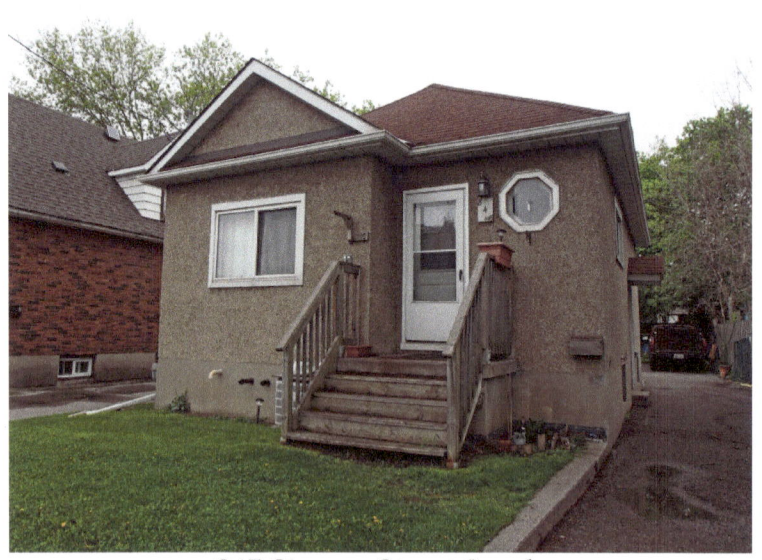
845 Simcoe Street South

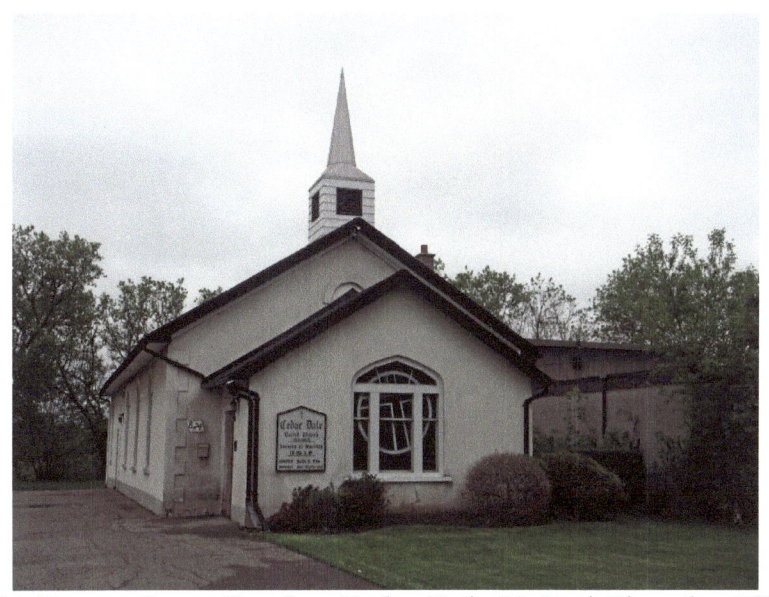

824 Simcoe Street South – Cedar Dale United Church - 1835

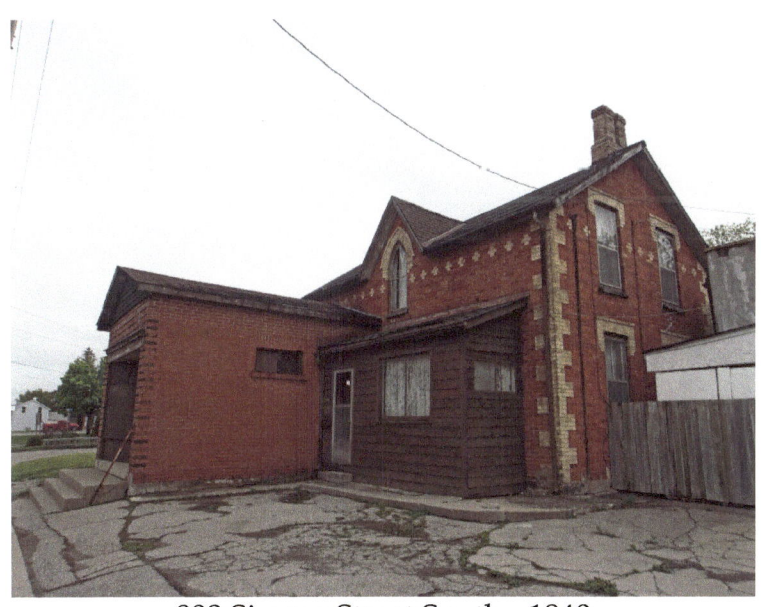

809 Simcoe Street South - 1840

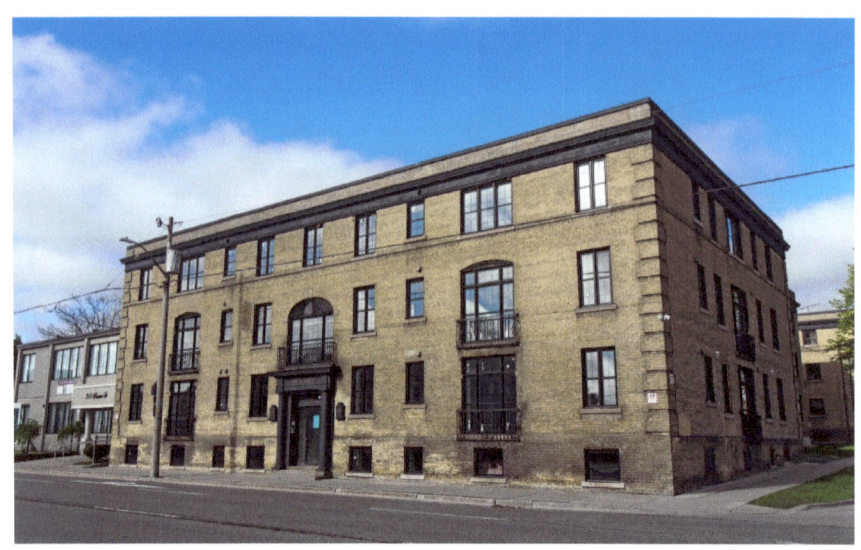
304 Simcoe Street South – The George Apartments - 1929

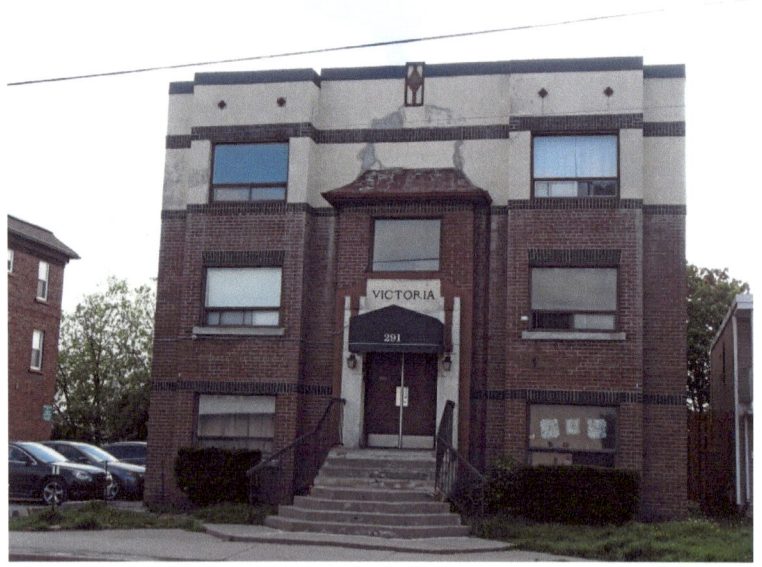
291 Simcoe Street South - Victoria Apartments - 1930

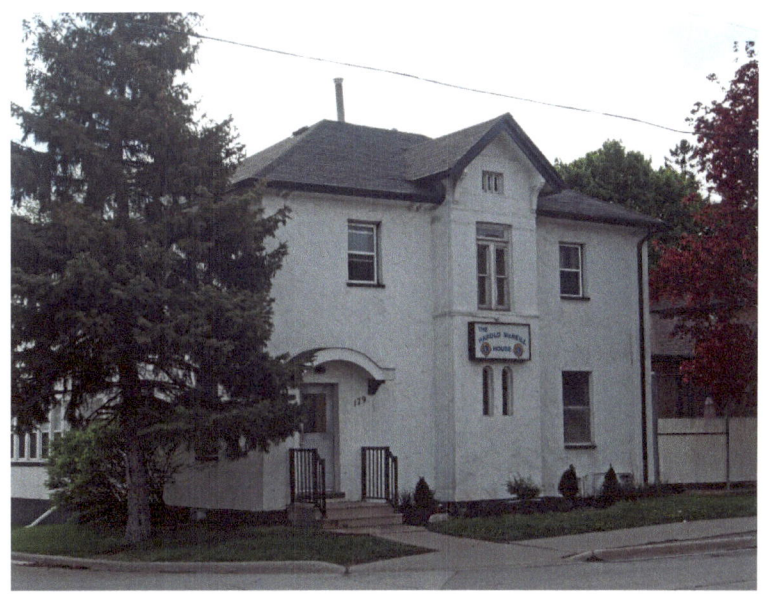

179 Simcoe Street South – The Harold McNeil House - 1860

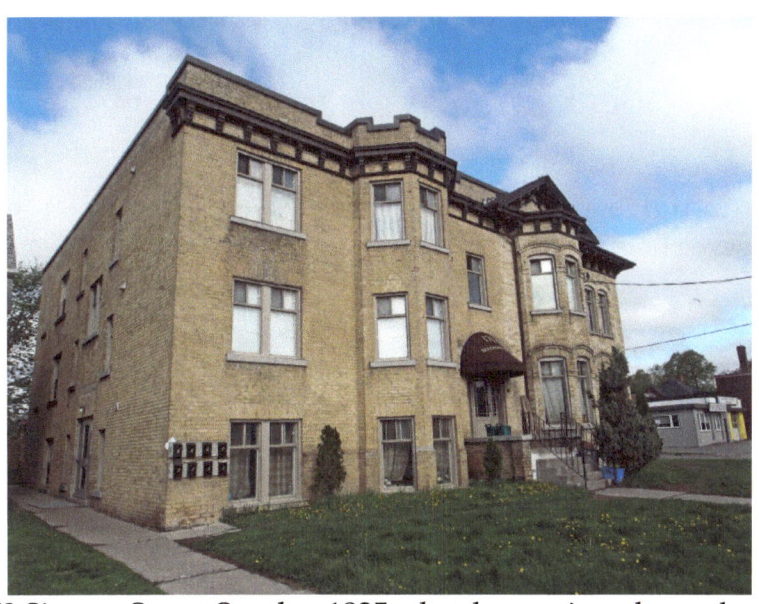

170 Simcoe Street South – 1925 – battlementing above three-storey bay window on left

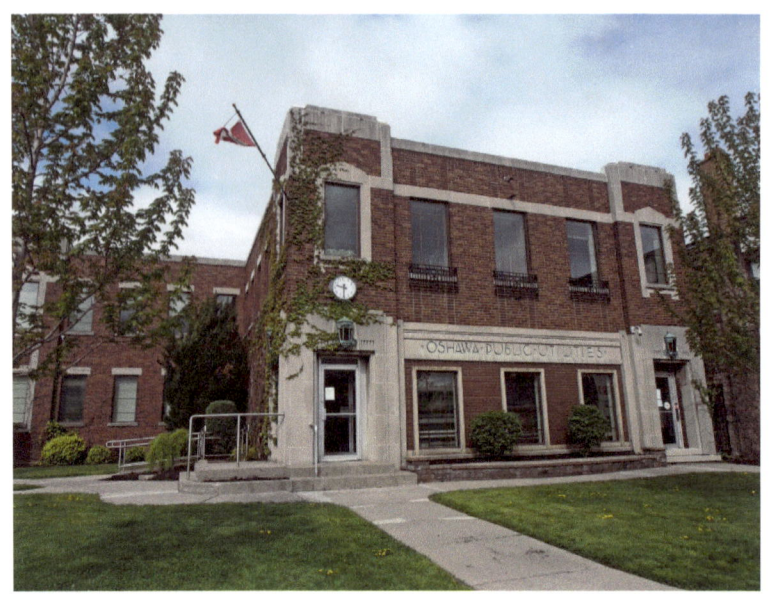

100 Simcoe Street South - Oshawa Public Utilities Commission - 1931

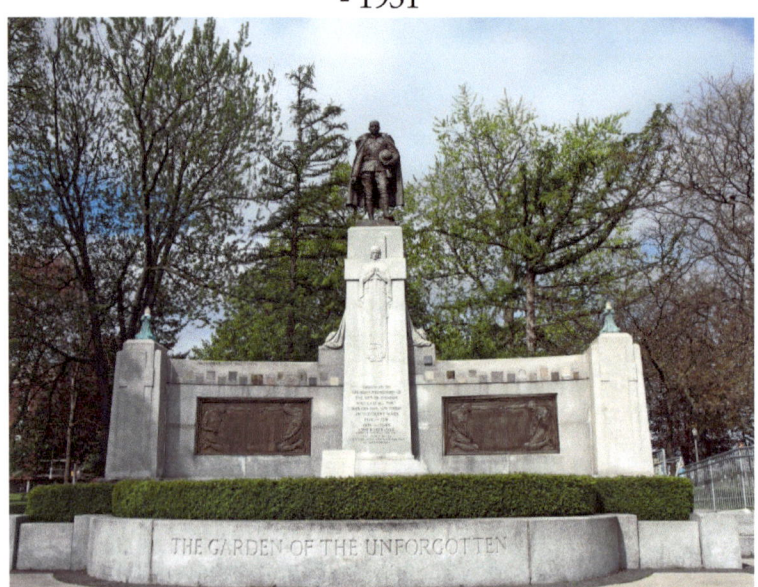

110 Simcoe Street South – Memorial Park – 1924 – The cenotaph includes stones collected from every allied country of WWI and every battlefield where Canadians died.

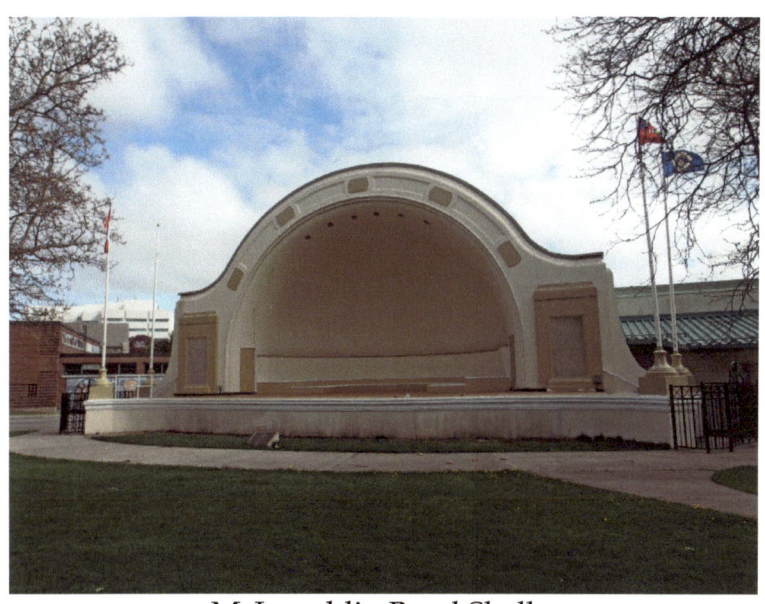

McLaughlin Band Shell -
A gift from Colonel R. S. McLaughlin (Oshawa industrialist and philanthropist) to the citizens of Oshawa – 1942

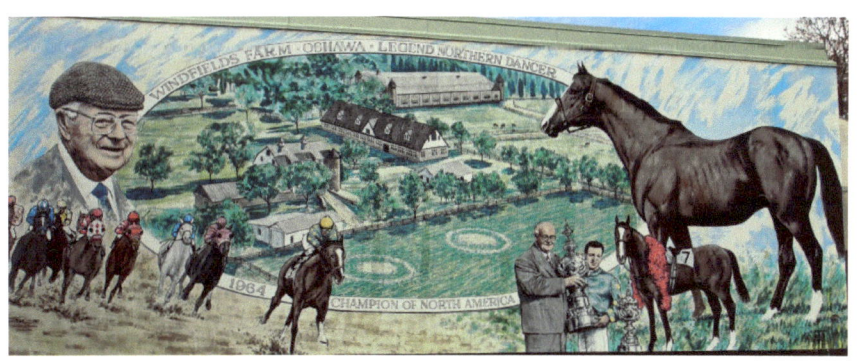

Park Mural – Windfields Farm Oshawa Legend Northern Dancer, 1964 Champion of North America

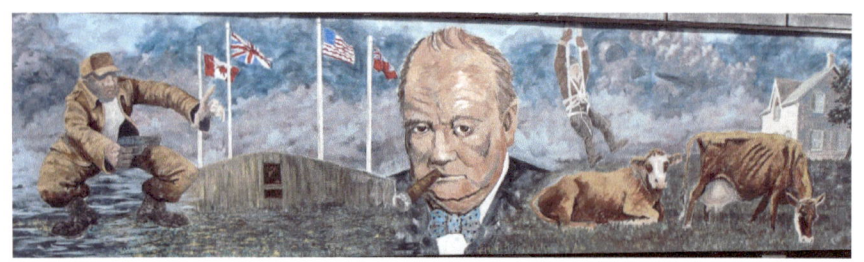

Mural on Metcalfe Street

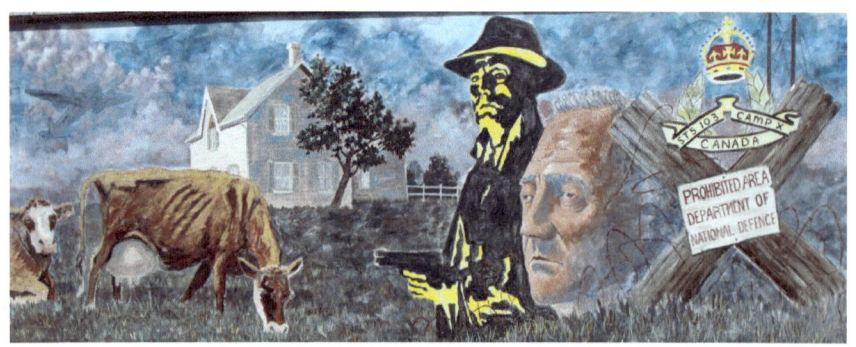

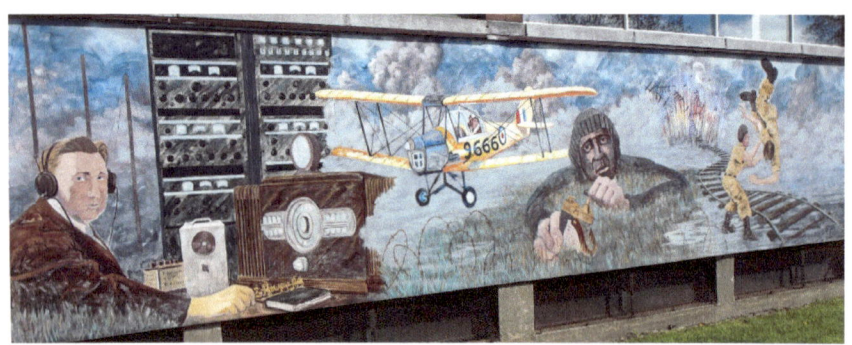

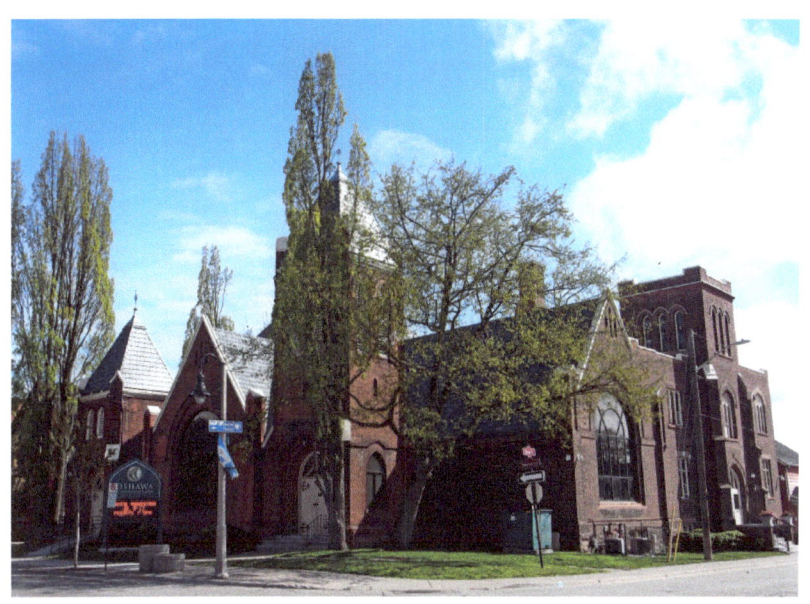

71 Simcoe Street South – Oshawa Community Church (former St. Andrew's United Church)

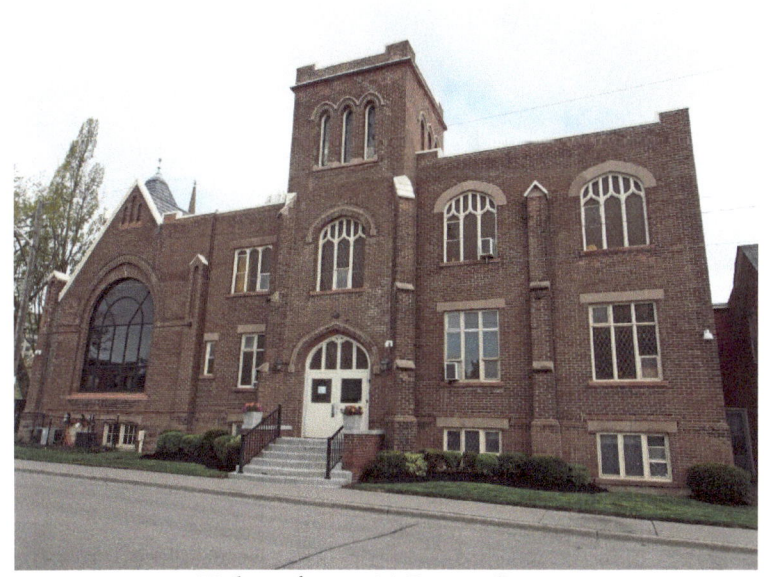

Taken from 16 Bruce Street

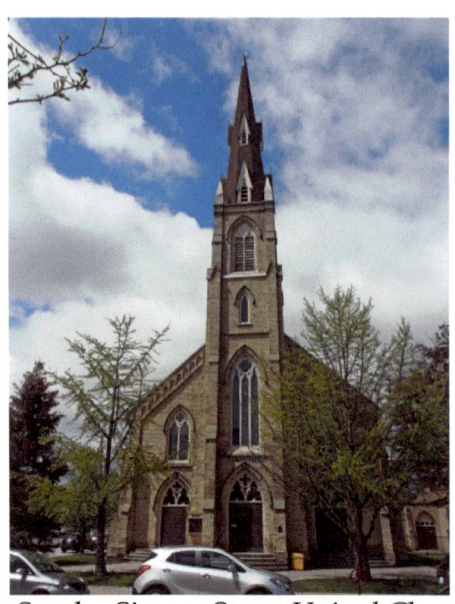

66 Simcoe Street South - Simcoe Street United Church – 1867-1868 – designed by architect firm of Gundy & Langley; Church steeple once stood 150 feet high but repaired after lightning strike to stand only 135 feet; the church holds 700-800 people

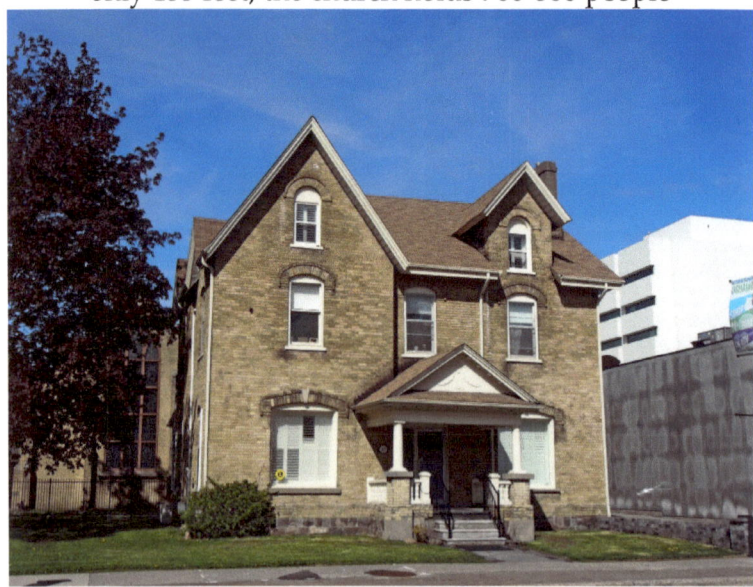

52 Simcoe Street South – 1954 – former church manse

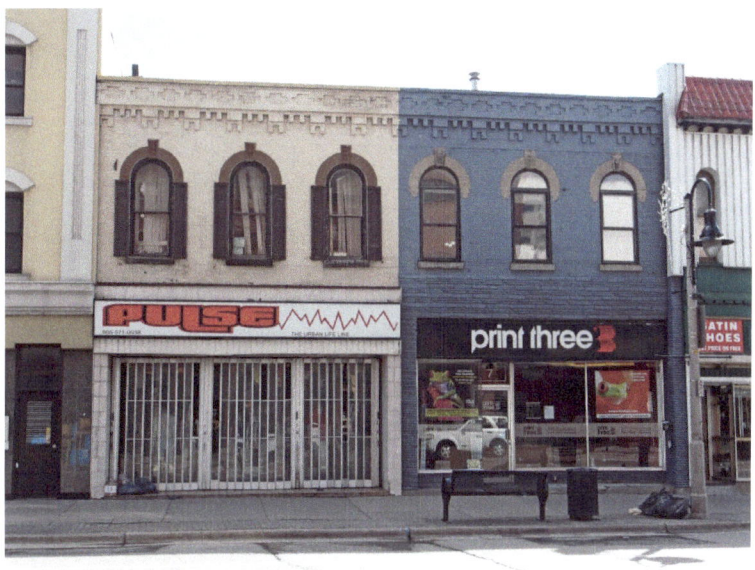

5-7 Simcoe Street South - 1860

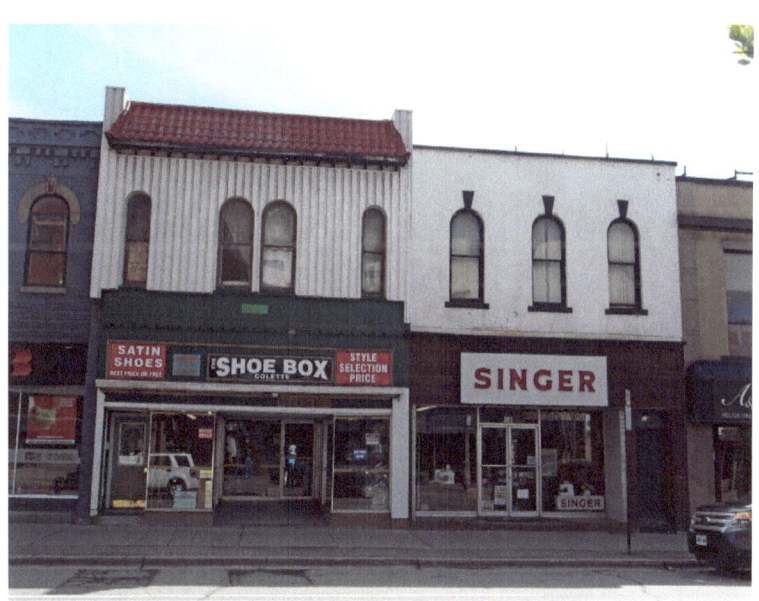

9-11 Simcoe Street South - 1860

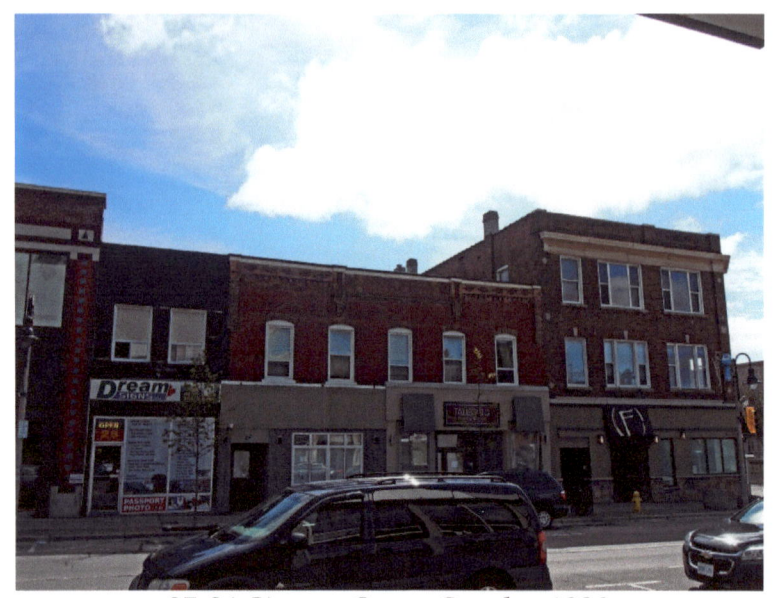
25-31 Simcoe Street South - 1920

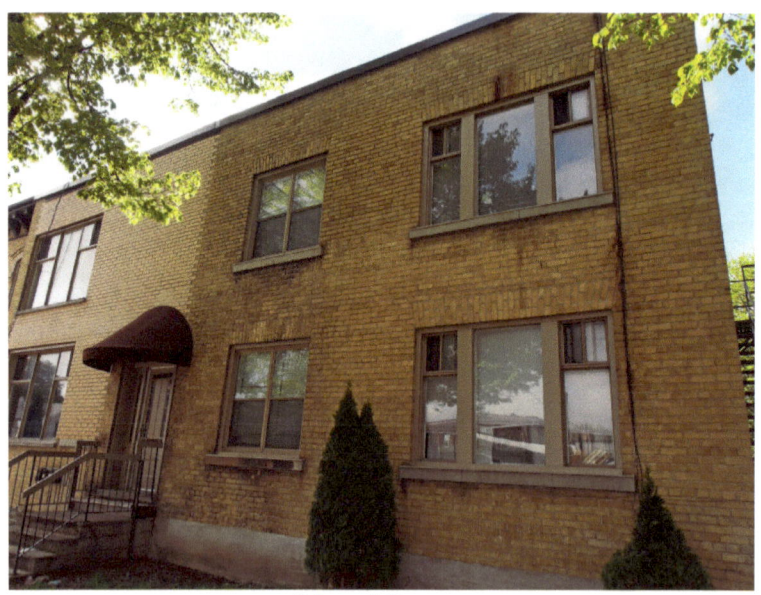
Lloyd Street

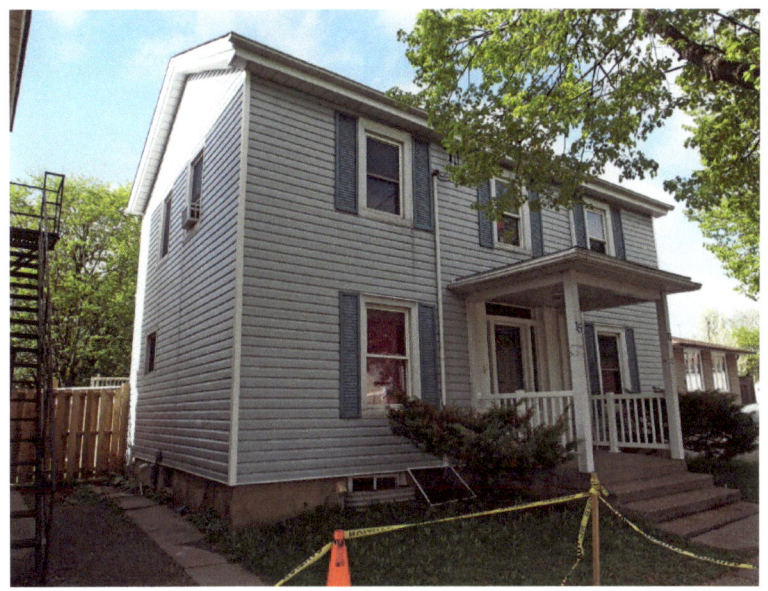

15 Lloyd Street - 1860

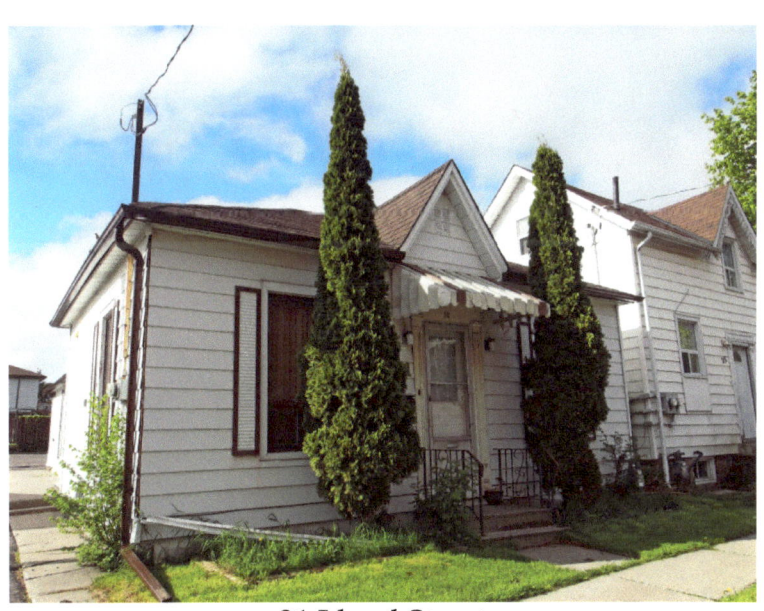

31 Lloyd Street

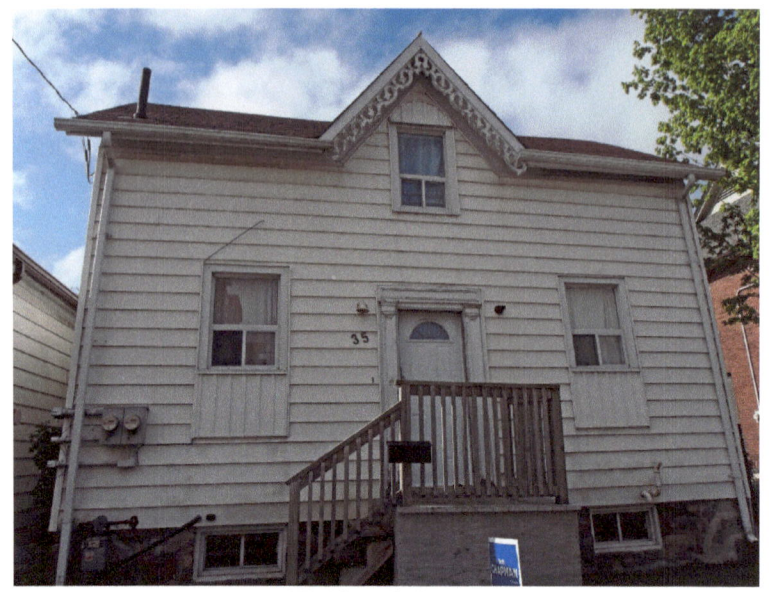
35 Lloyd Street

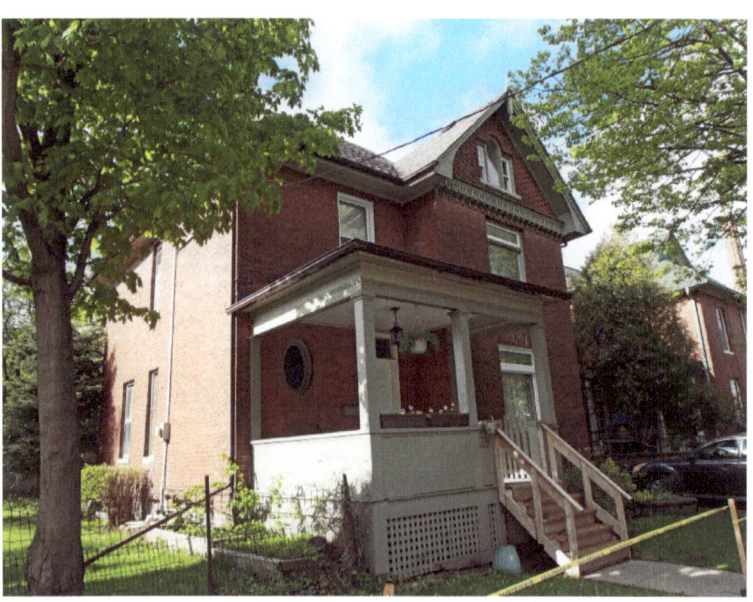
39 Lloyd Street

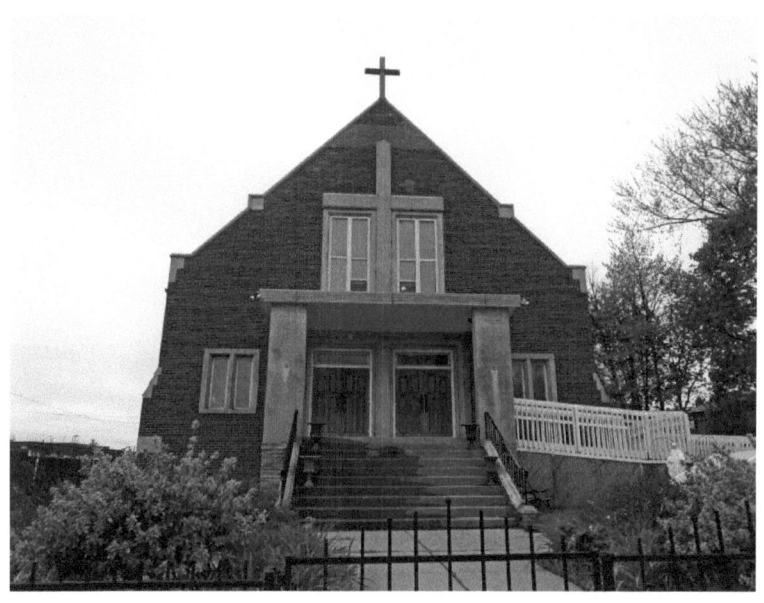

1314 Oxford Street – St. Philip's Roman Catholic Church - 1900

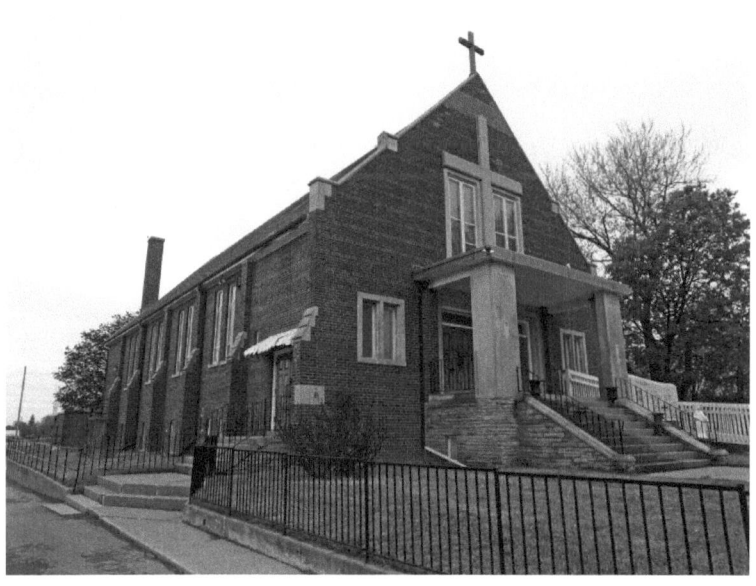

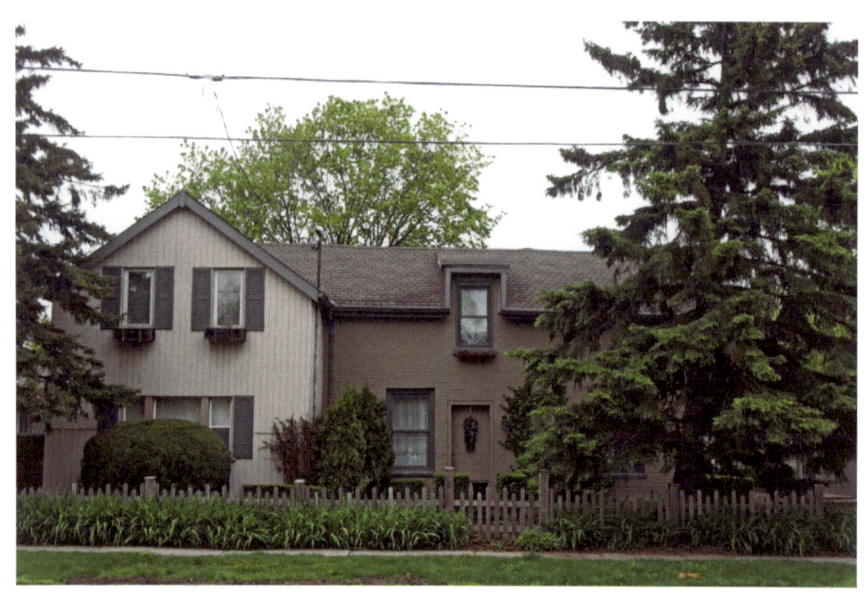

555-557 Cubert Street - 1900

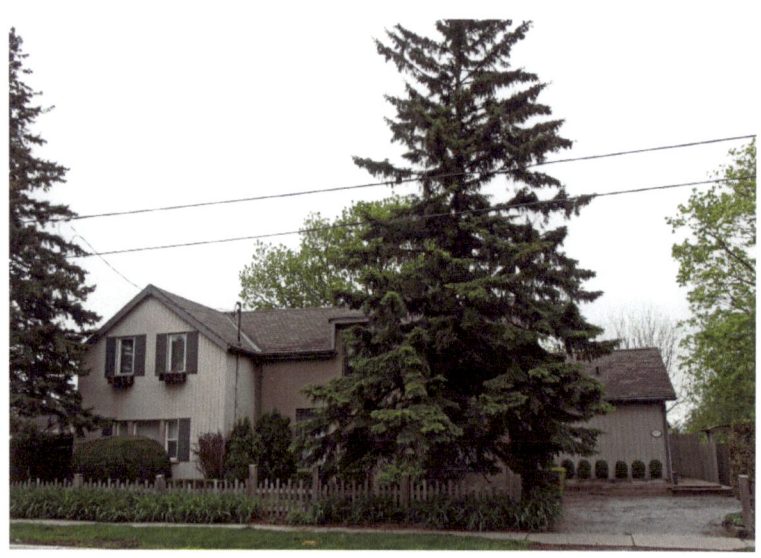

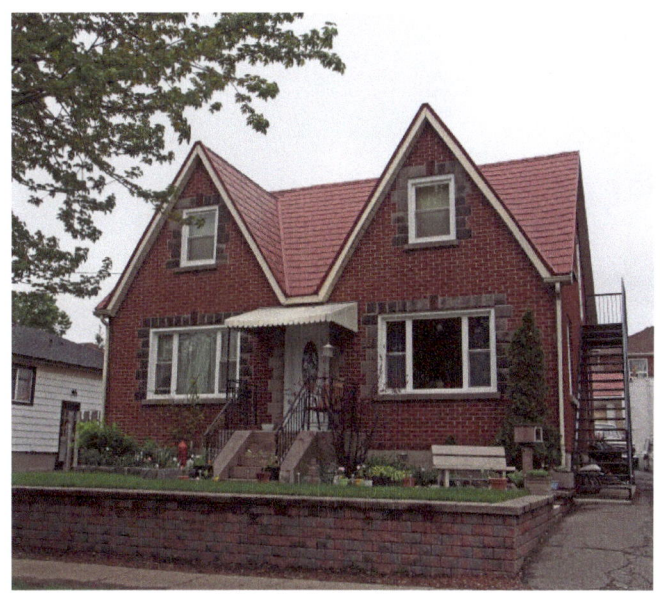

564 Cubert Street

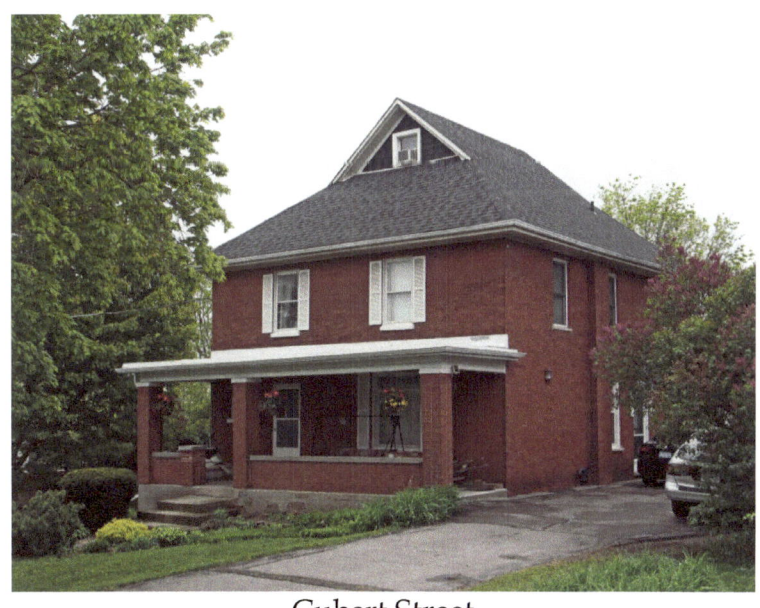

Cubert Street

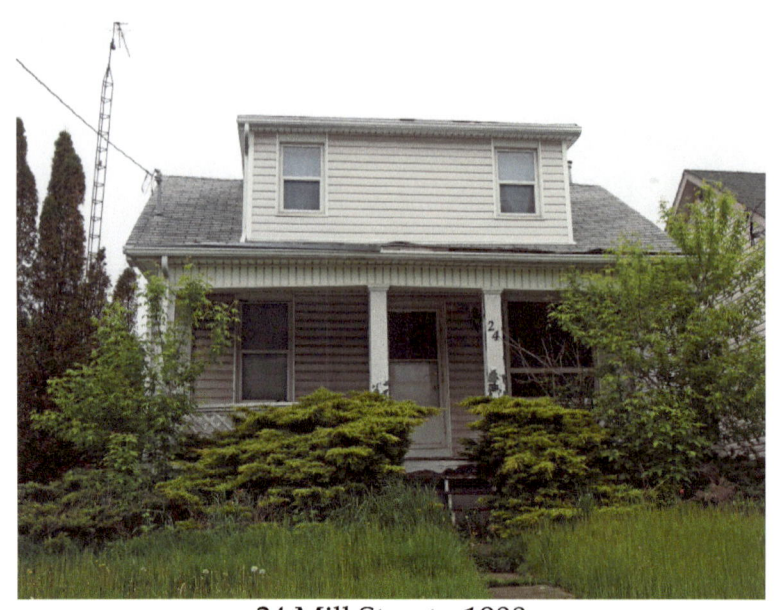

24 Mill Street - 1900

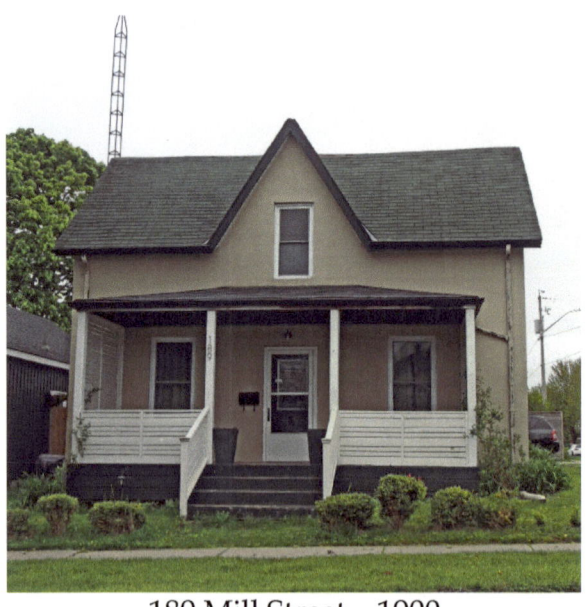

189 Mill Street – 1900

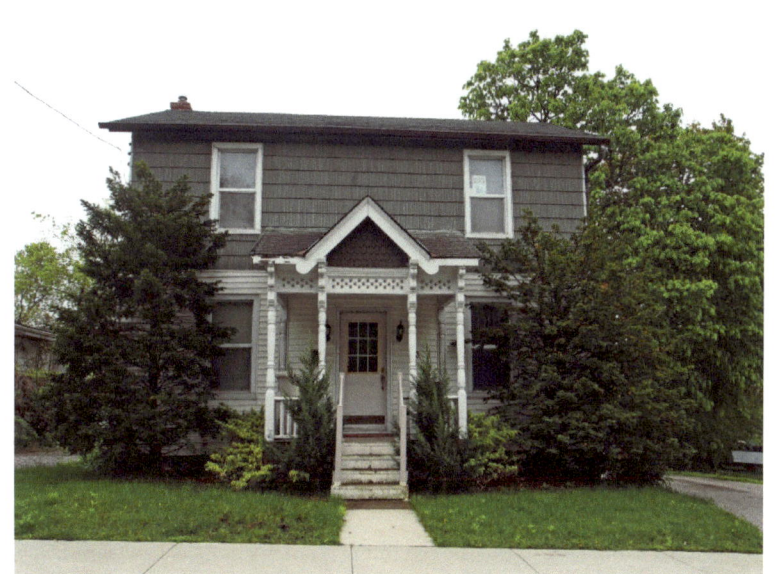

33 Avenue Street - 1900

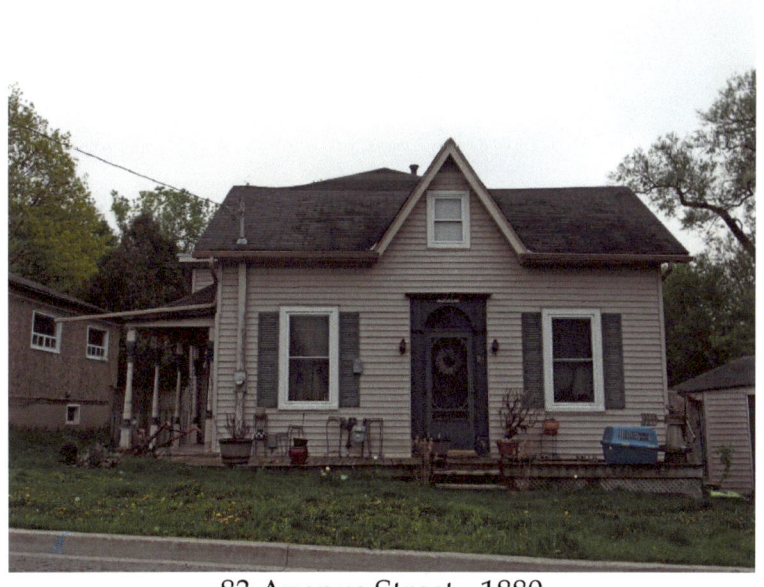

83 Avenue Street - 1880

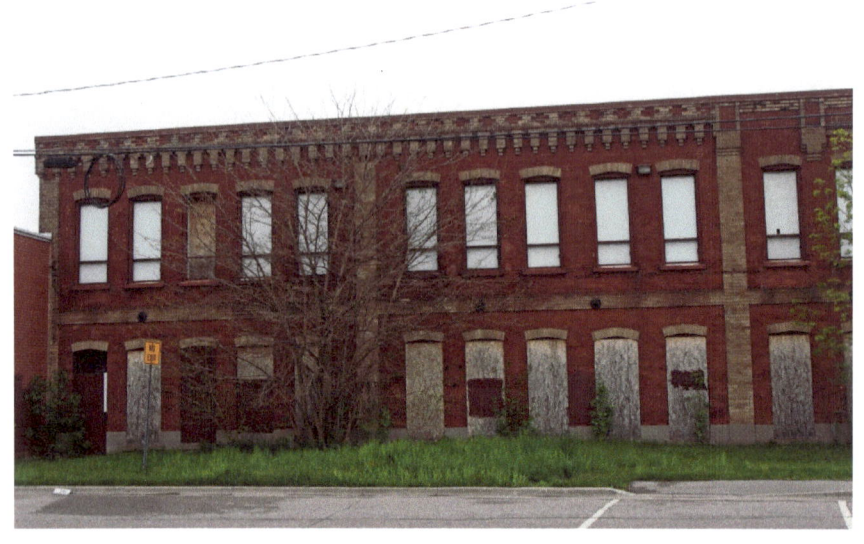

1500 Howard Street – Ontario Malleable Iron – c. 1880 – bevelled dentil molding, pilasters, banding

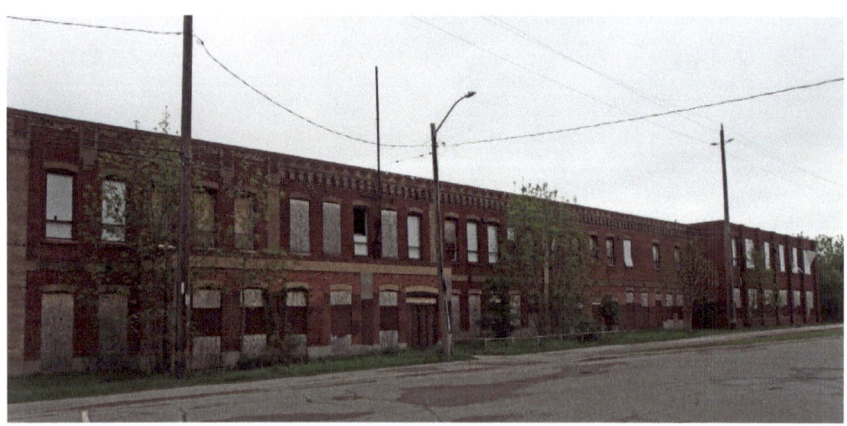

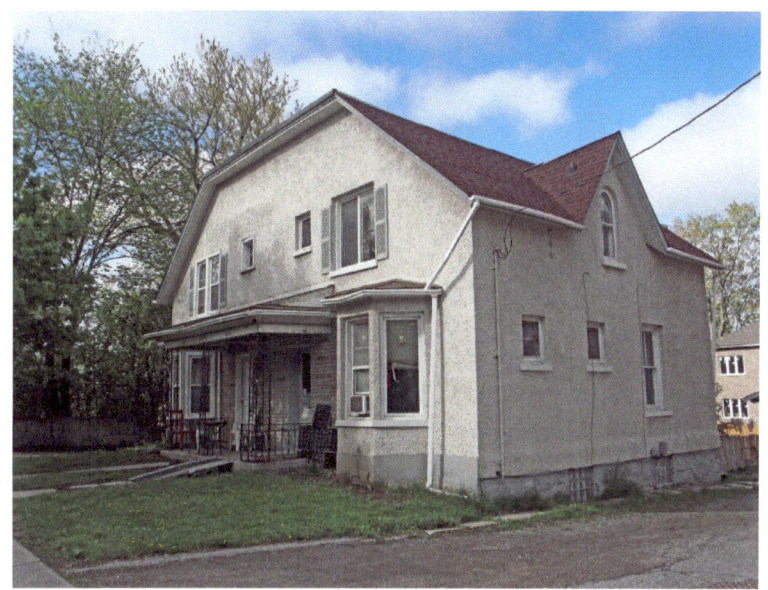

214-216 Centre Street South - 1920

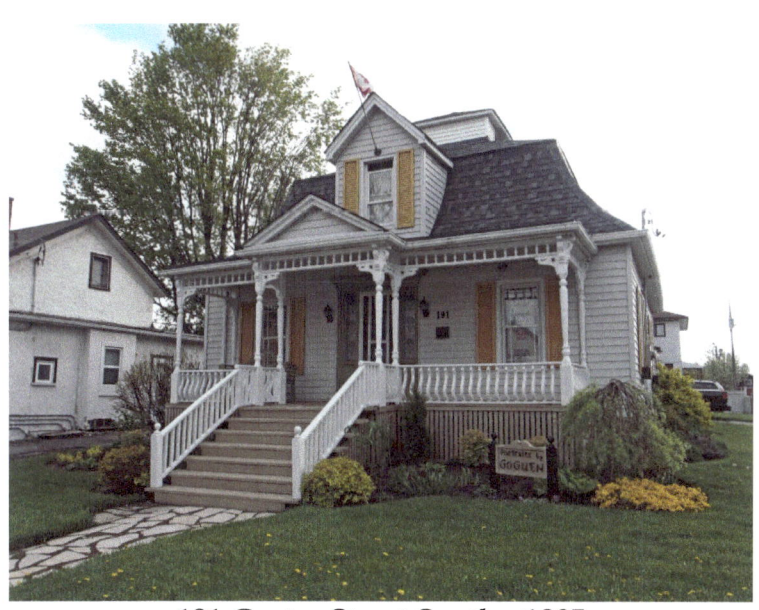

191 Centre Street South - 1905

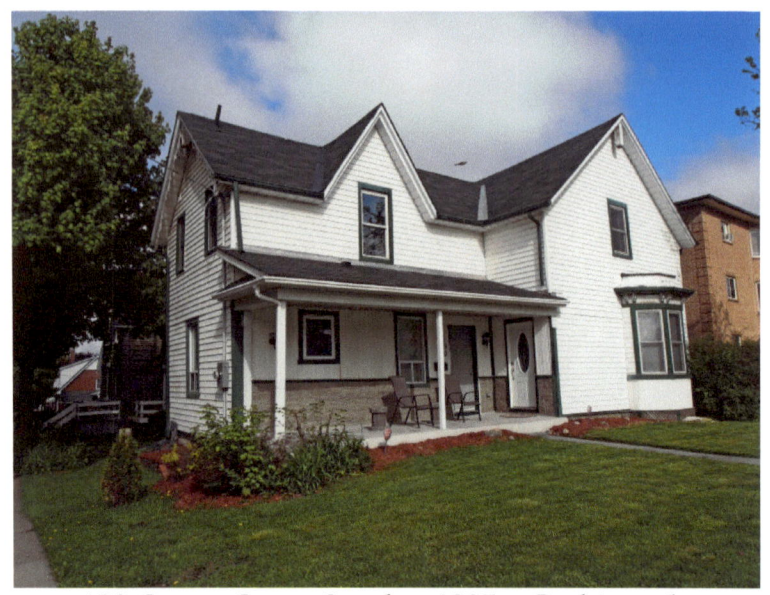

190 Centre Street South – 1885 – Gothic style

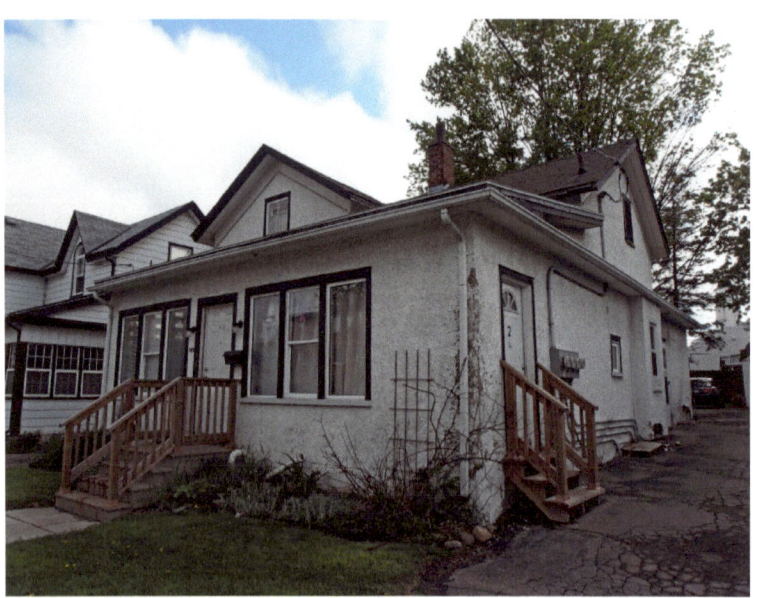

185 Centre Street South

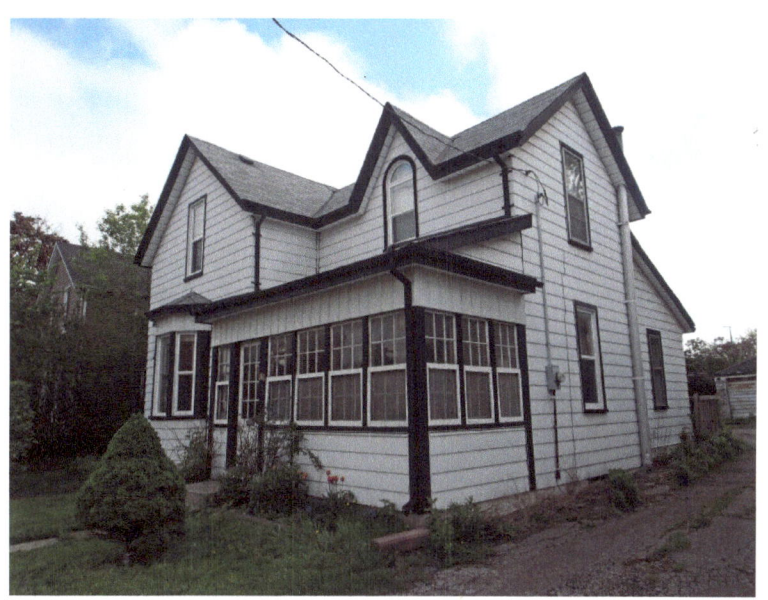

179 Centre Street South – 1875 – Gothic style

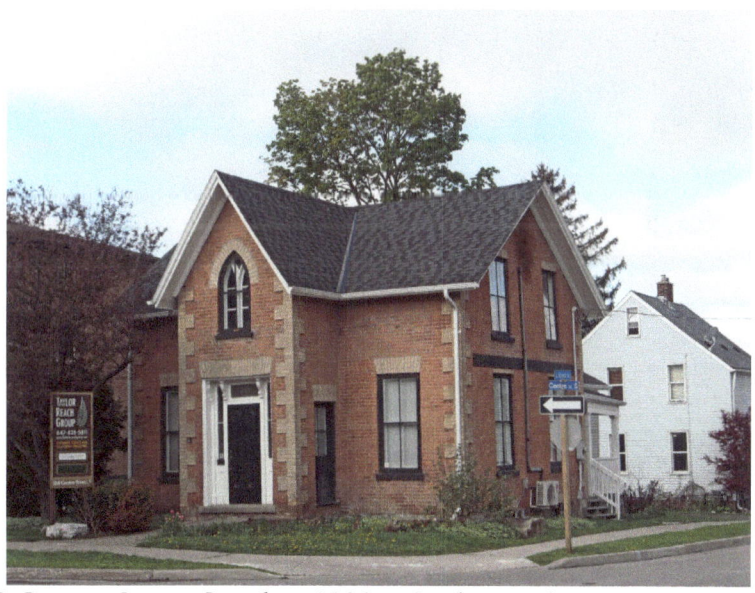

168 Centre Street South – 1890 – Gothic style – corner quoins, dichromatic brickwork

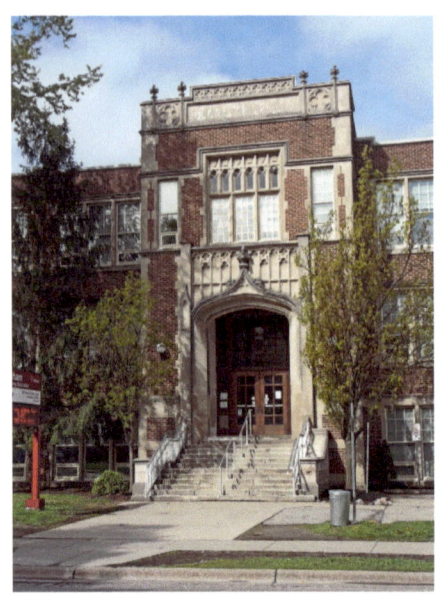

120 Centre Street South - EA Lovell School - 1924

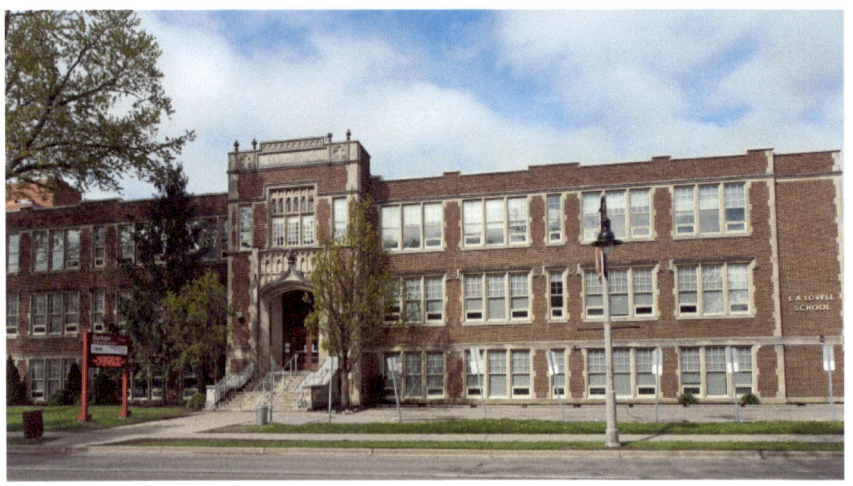

Neo-Gothic style

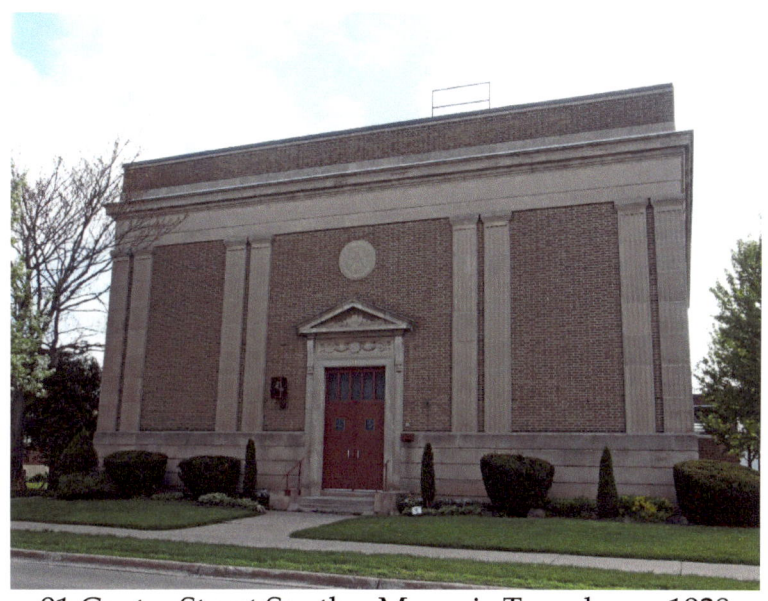

91 Centre Street South – Masonic Temple – c. 1928

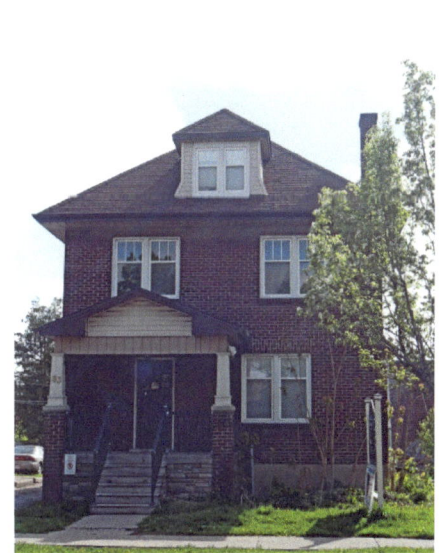

83 Centre Street South
c. 1923

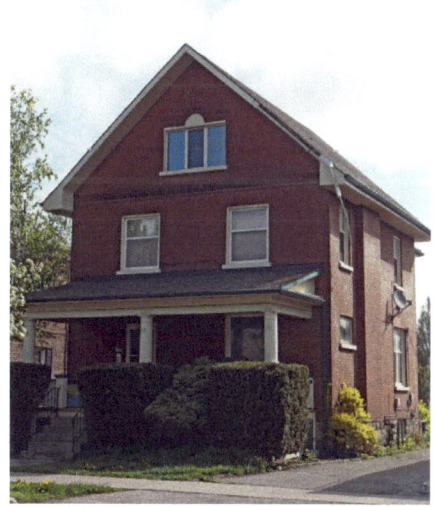

79 Centre Street South
c. 1925

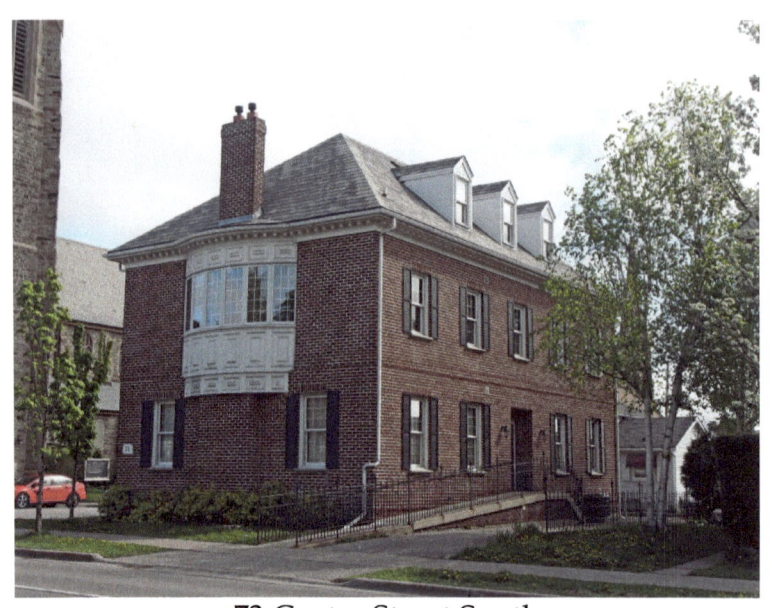

73 Centre Street South

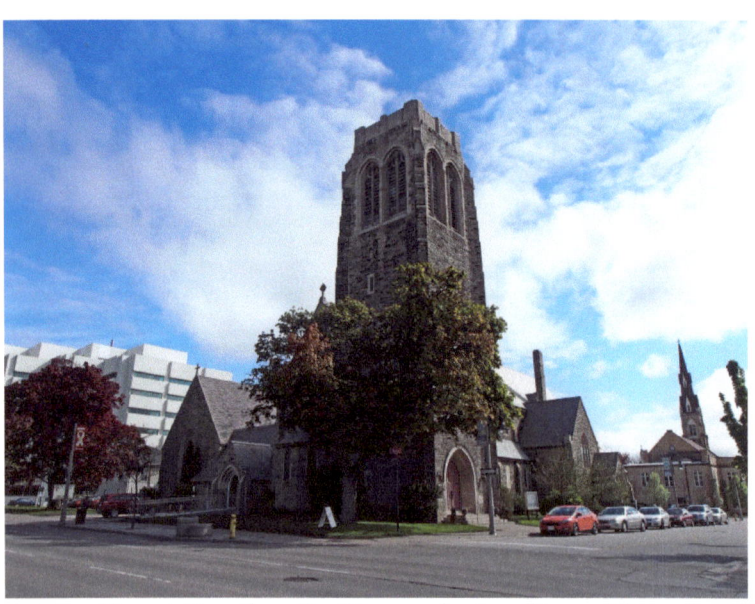

51 Centre Street South – St. George's Anglican Church - 1922

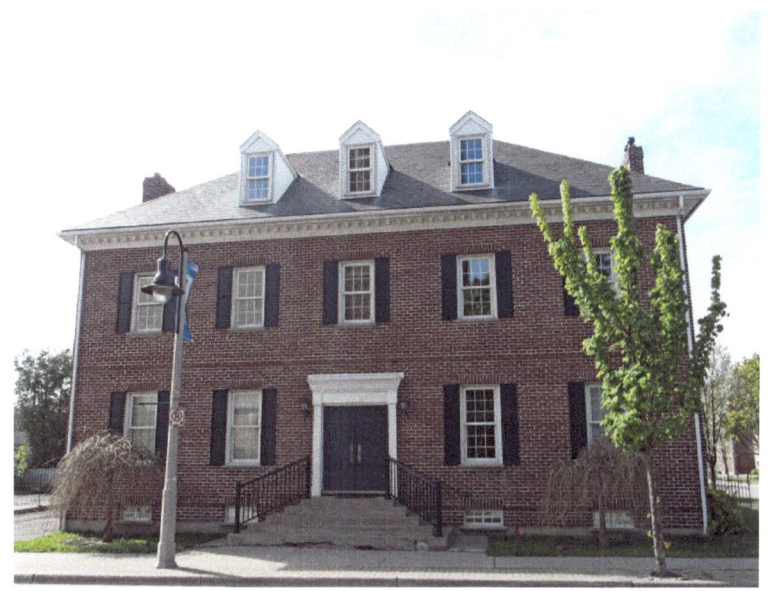
Centre Street South – Georgian style, dormers

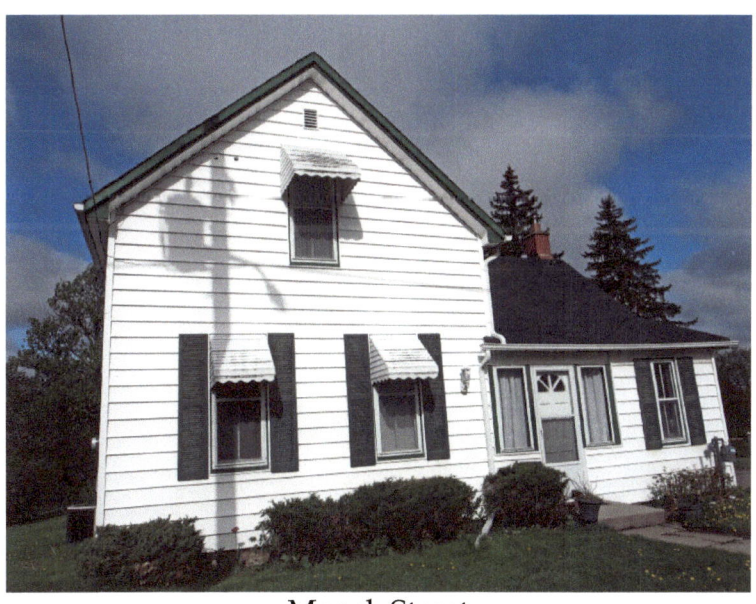
Monck Street

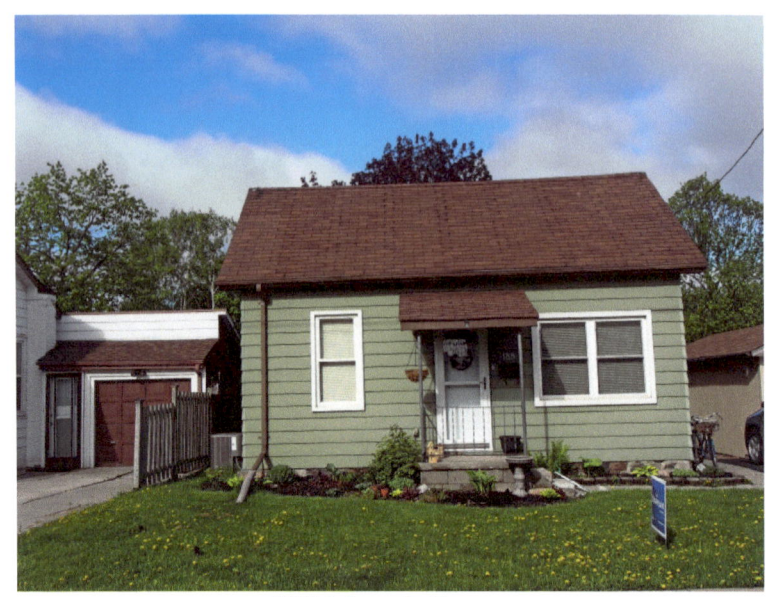
188 Monck Street

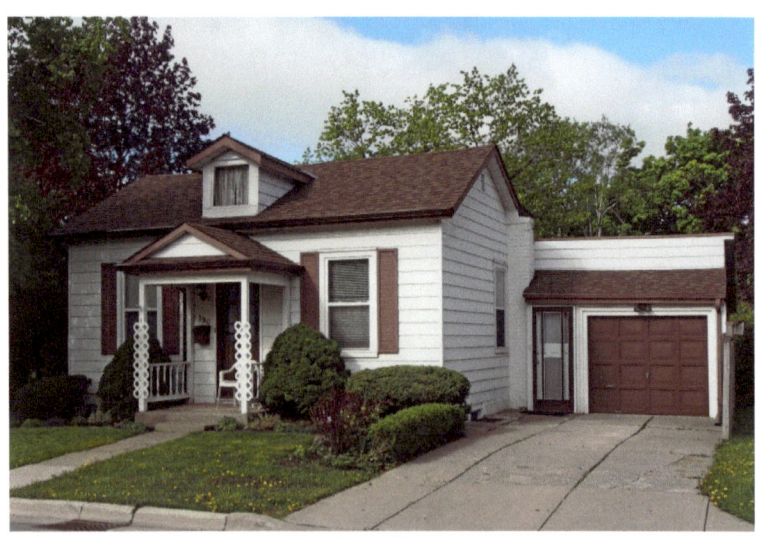
190 Monck Street

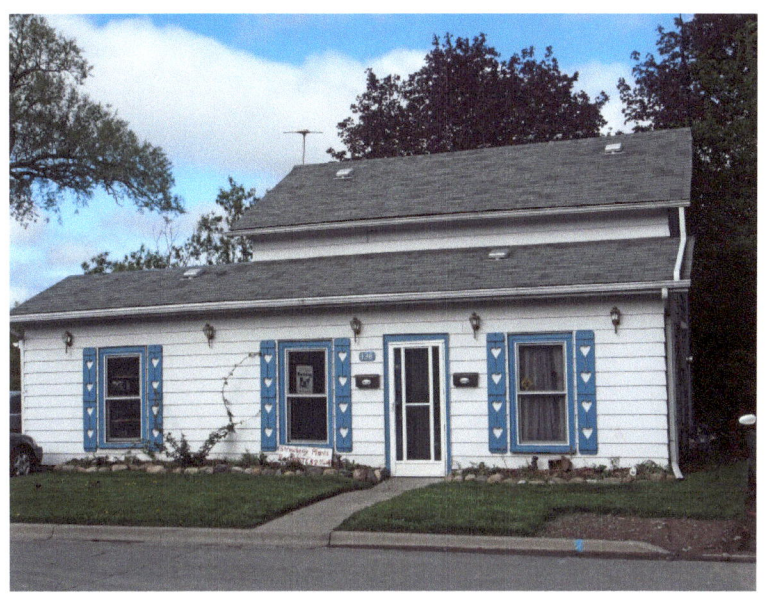

198 Monck Street

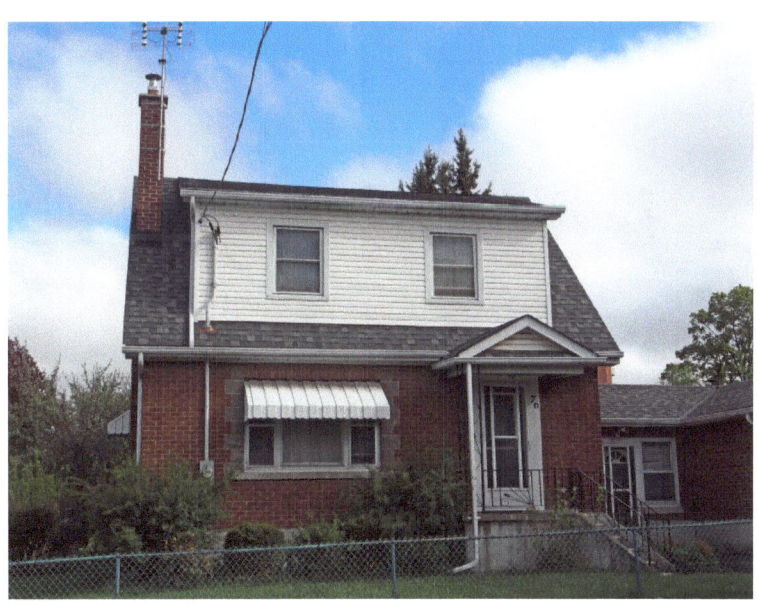

76 McGrigor Street

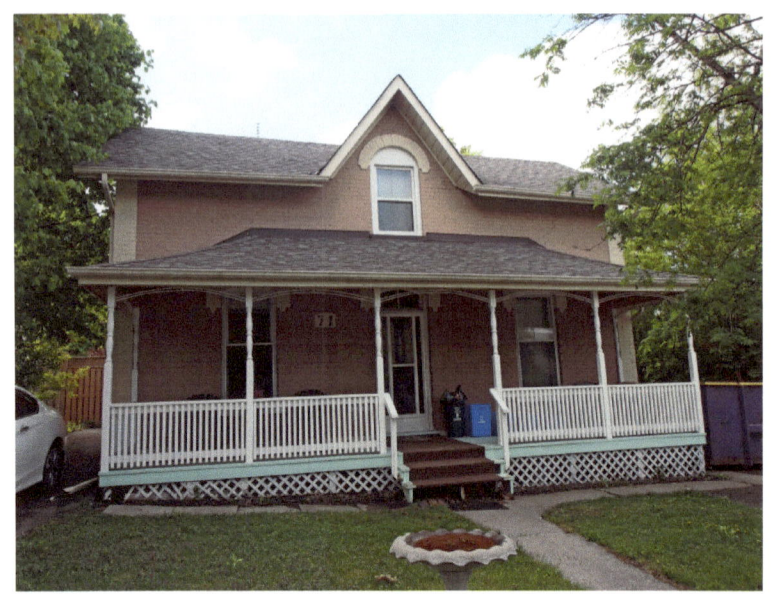

71 McGrigor Street - 1900

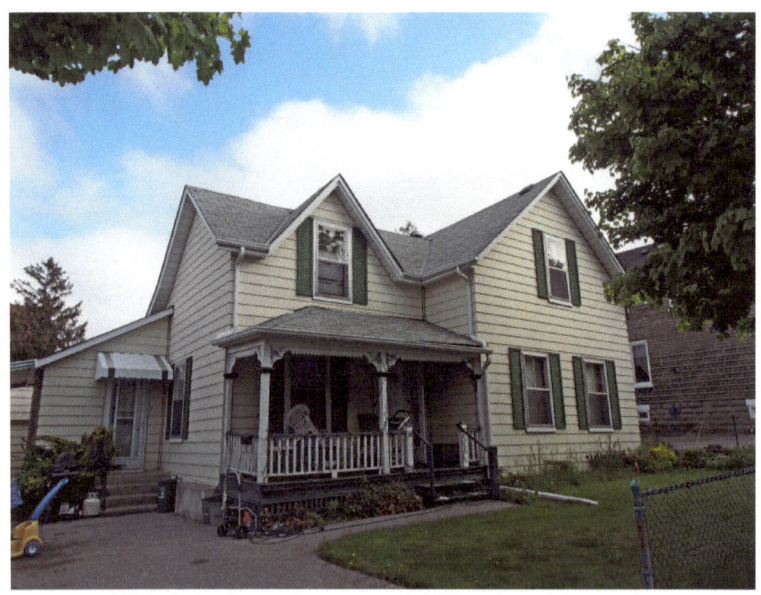

70 McGrigor Street – 1875 – Gothic style

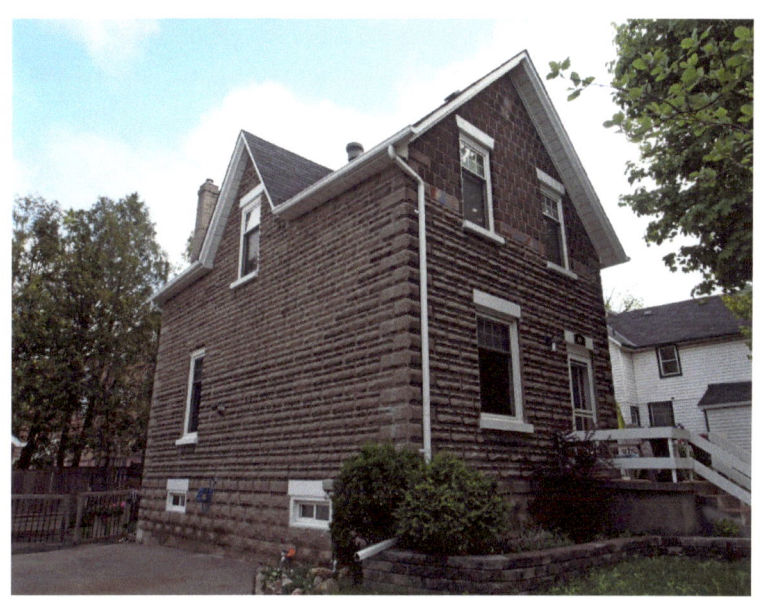

66 McGrigor Street - 1915

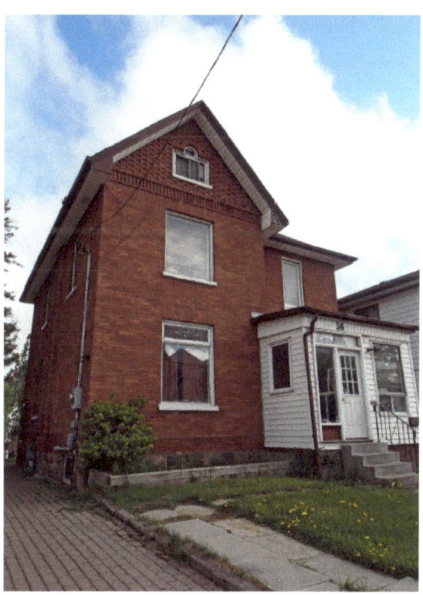

36 McGrigor Street - 1905

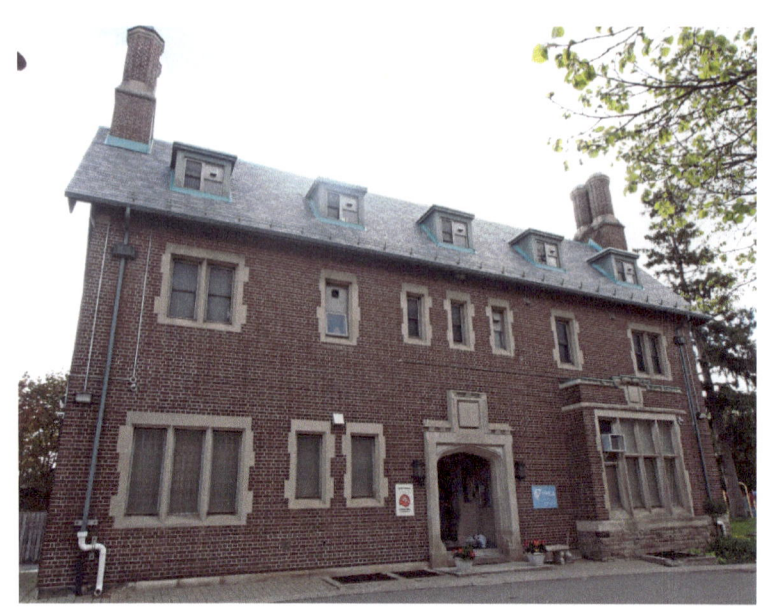

33 McGrigor Street – Adelaide House YWCA – c. 1920

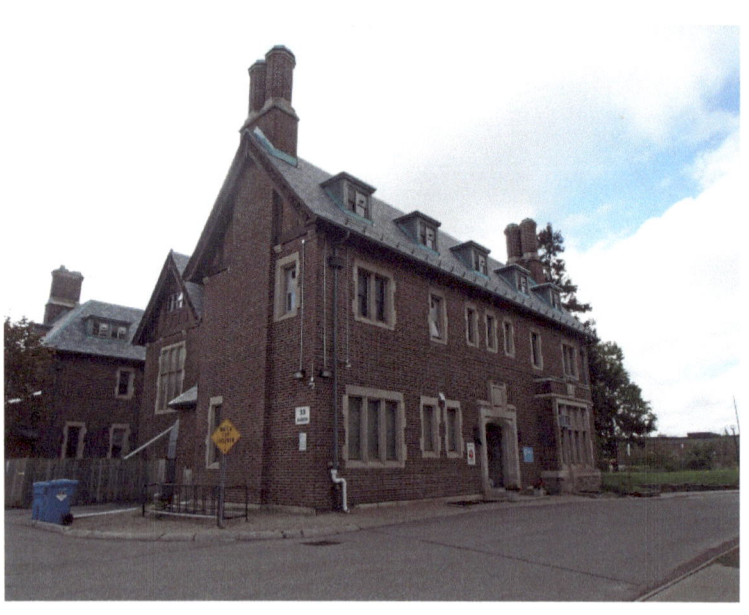

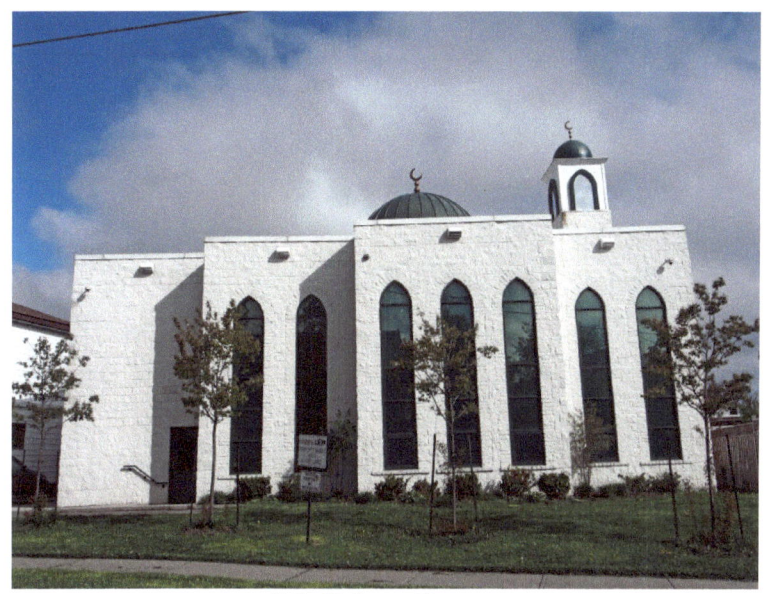

McGrigor Street

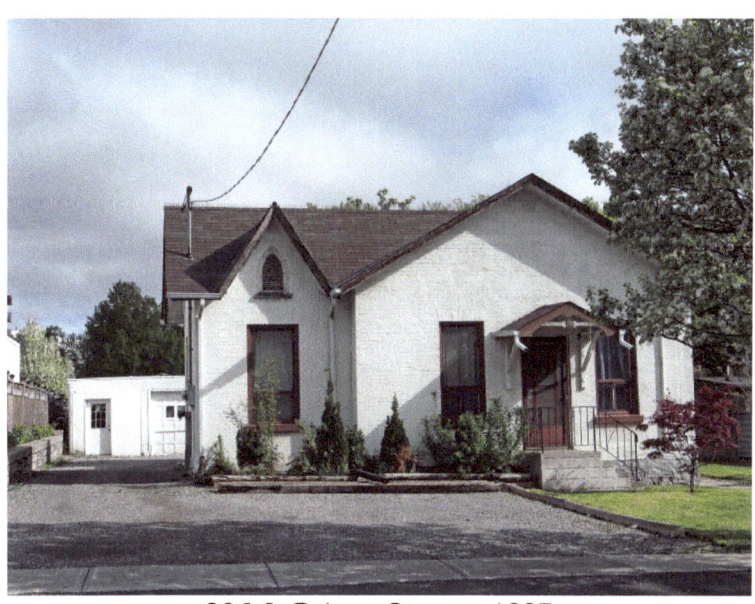

20 McGrigor Street - 1885

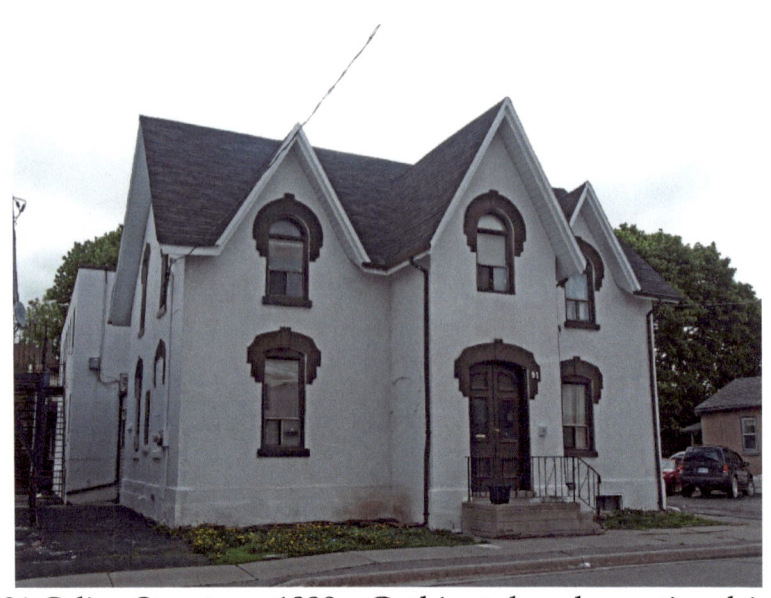

91 Celina Street – c. 1890 – Gothic style – decorative drip molds with keystones around windows and doors

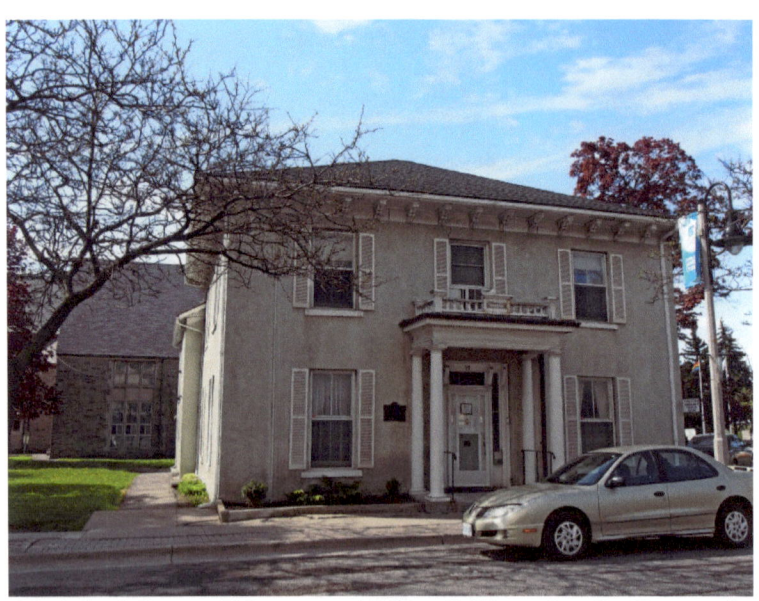

39 Athol Street West – c. 1858 - Offices for St George's Memorial Anglican Church – cornice brackets, second floor balcony above pillared entrance

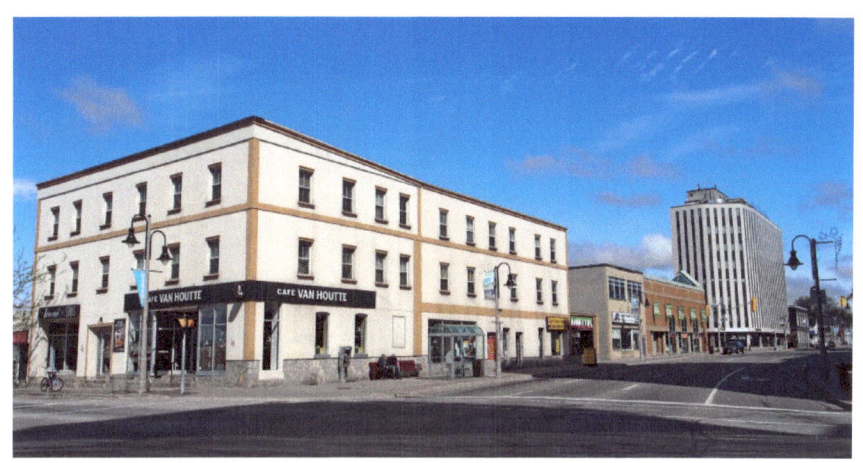

62 King Street West - Café Van Houtte

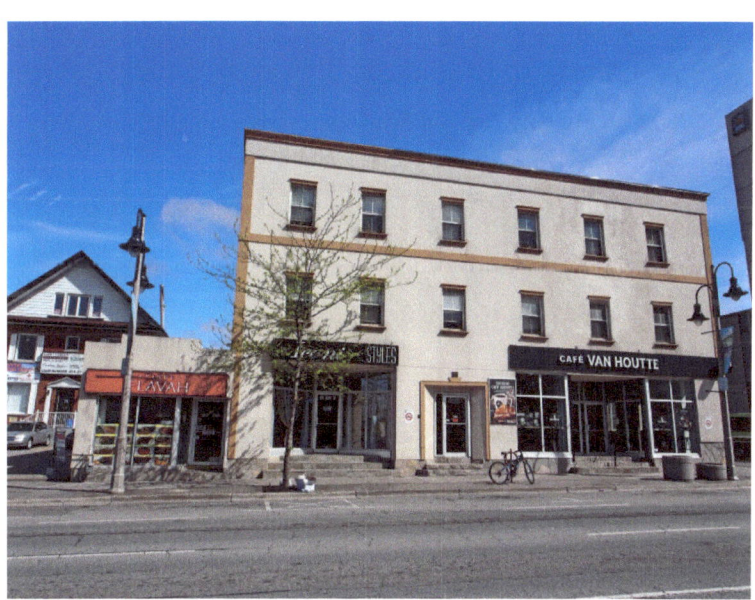

66-68 King Street West – Oshawa House Hotel - 1838

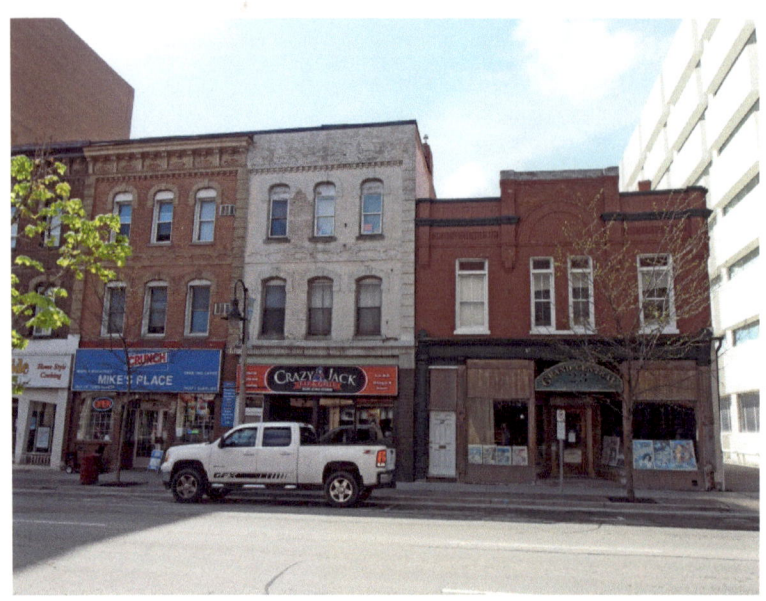

17-23 King Street West - William J. Cowan Block - 1860

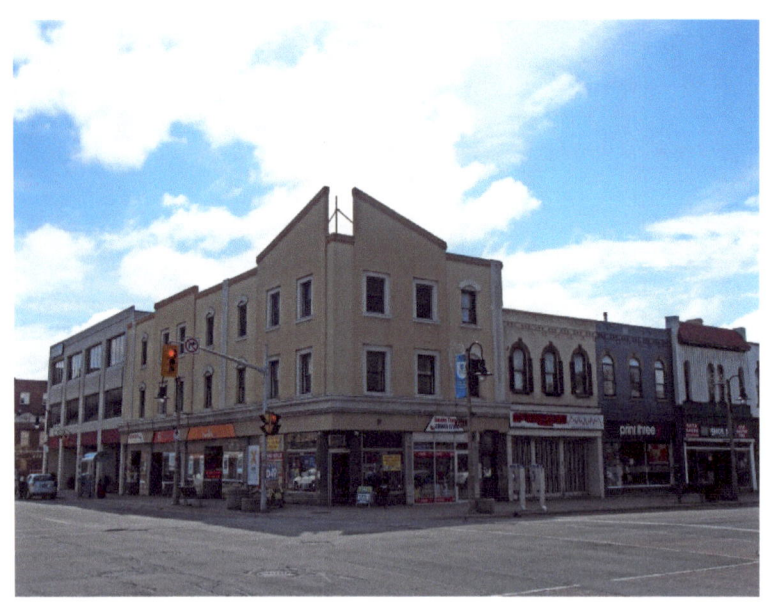

1 Simcoe Street South at King Street - 1860

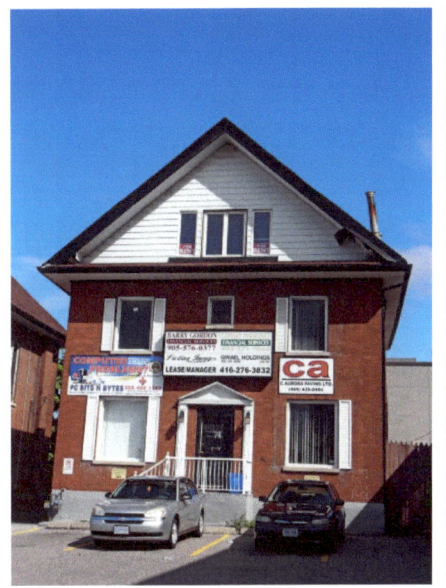
74 King Street West

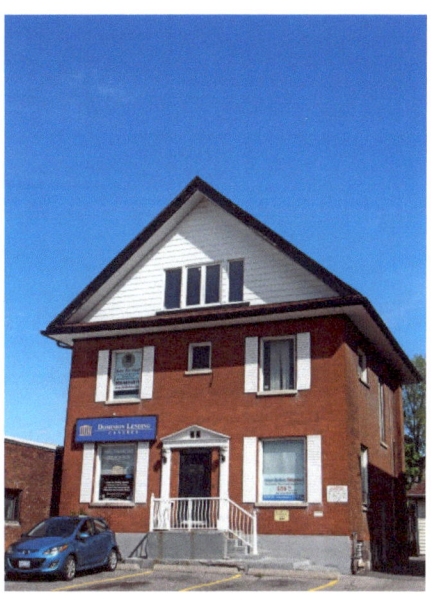
76 King Street West

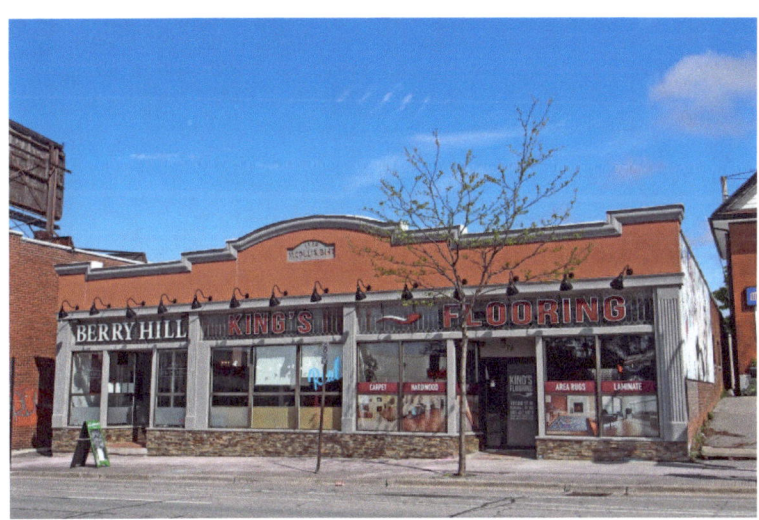
78-82 King Street West – M. Collis Building – 1928 – stepped parapet

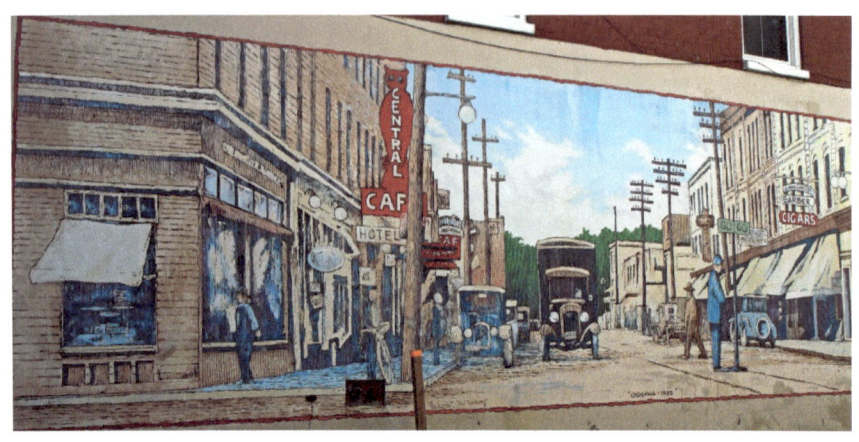

Mural

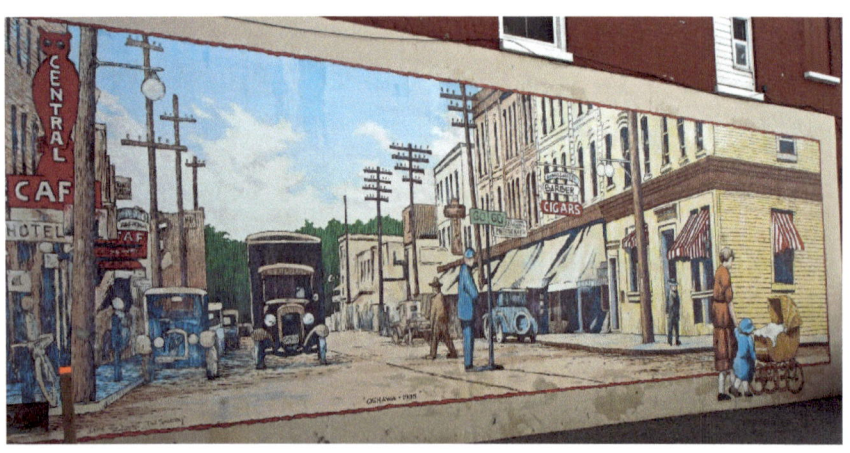

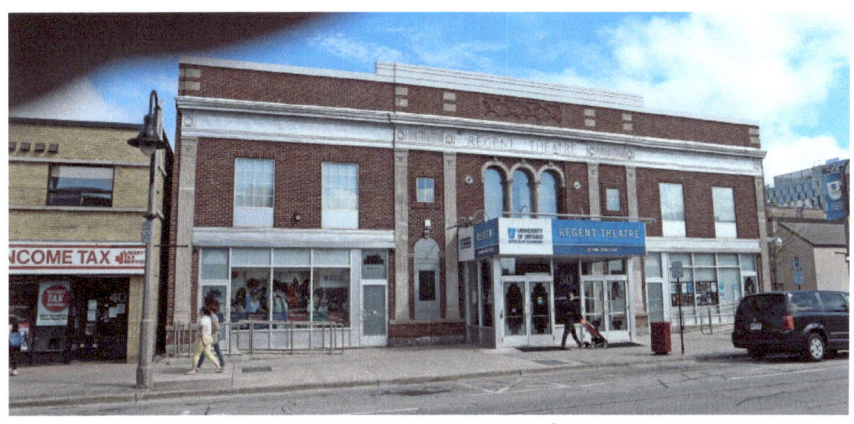

50 King Street East – Regent Theatre - 1919

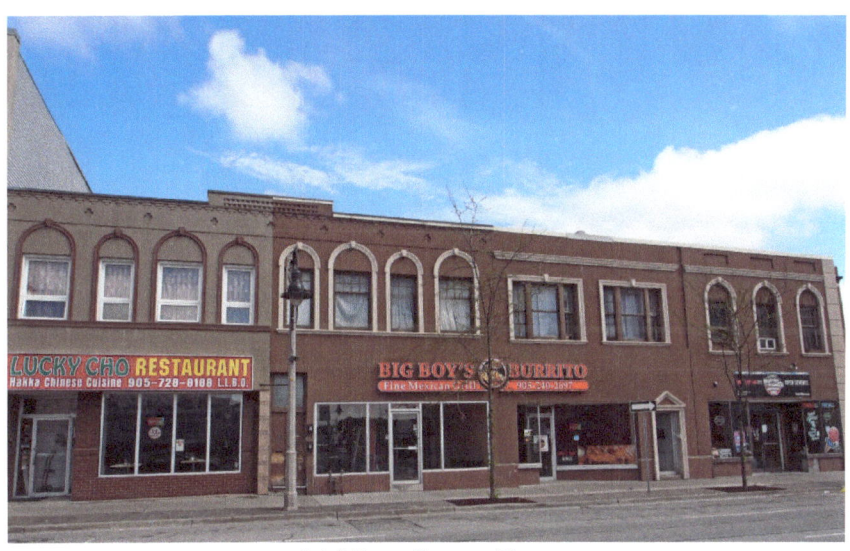

24 King Street East

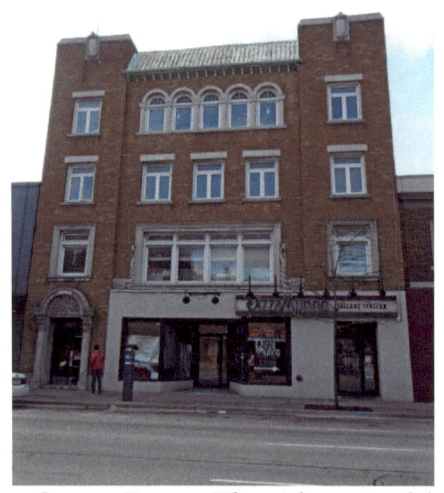

35-37 King Street East – The Alger Building - 1928

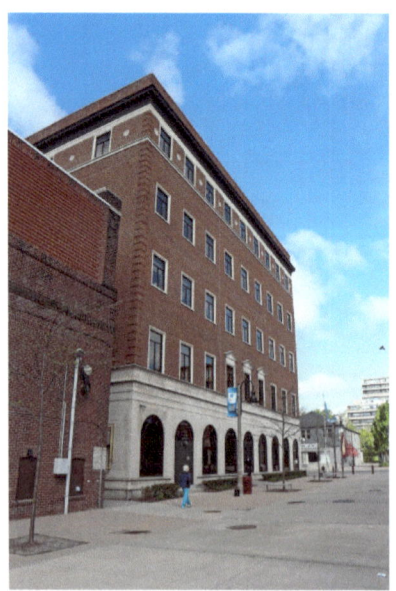

Victoria Street

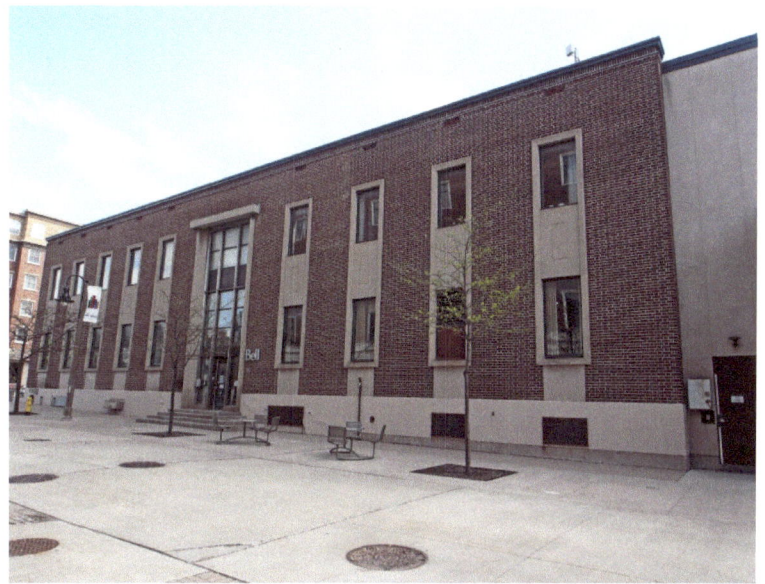

15 Victoria Street – Bell Building

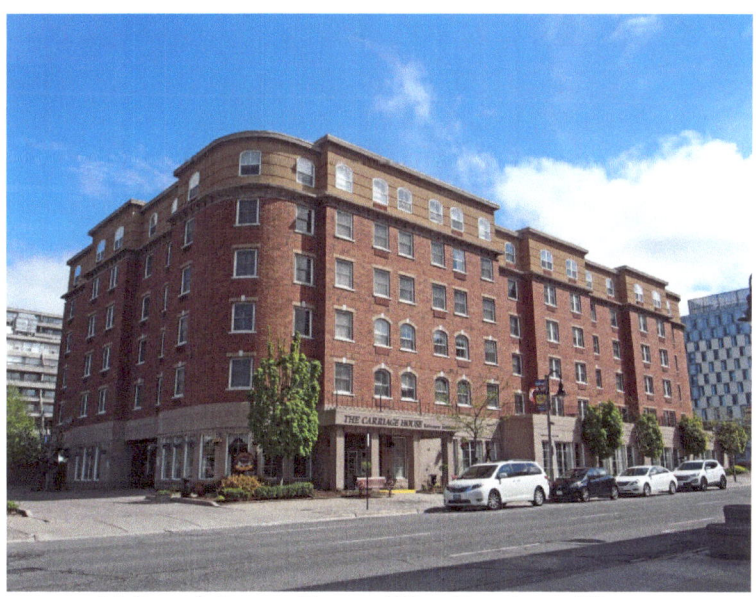

60 Bond Street East – The Carriage House

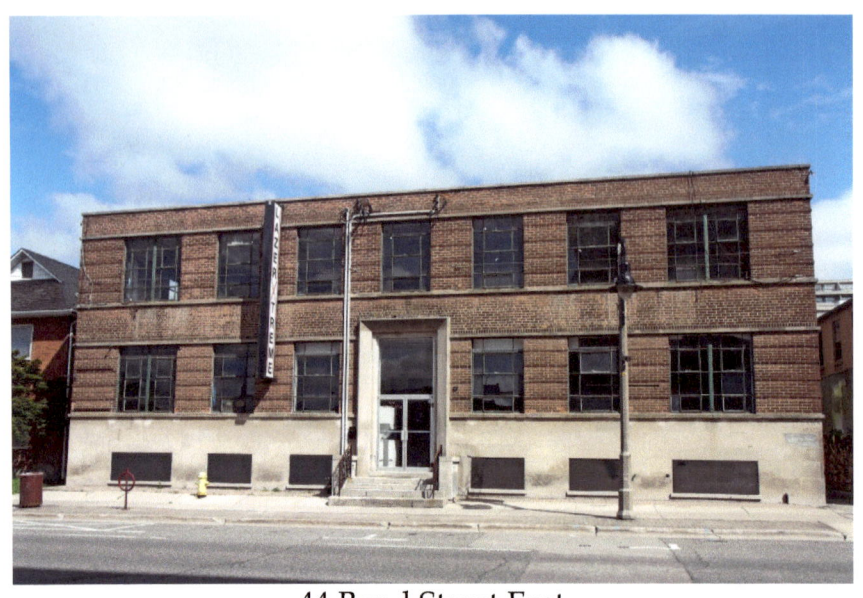

44 Bond Street East

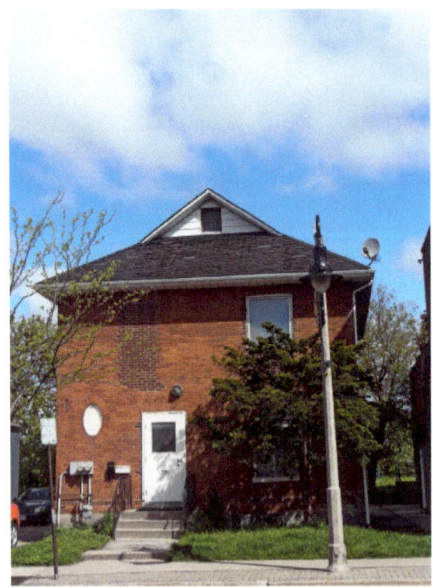

Bond Street East

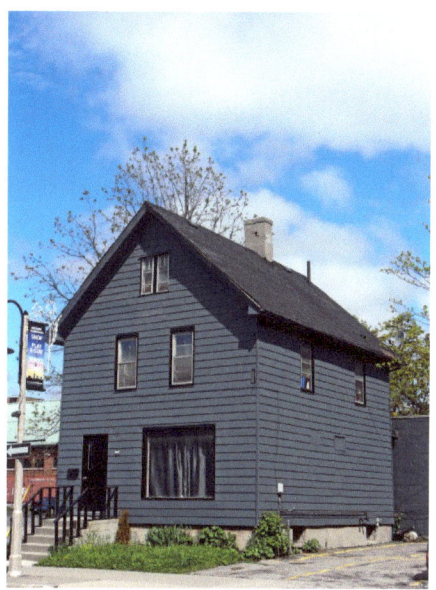

32 Bond Street East

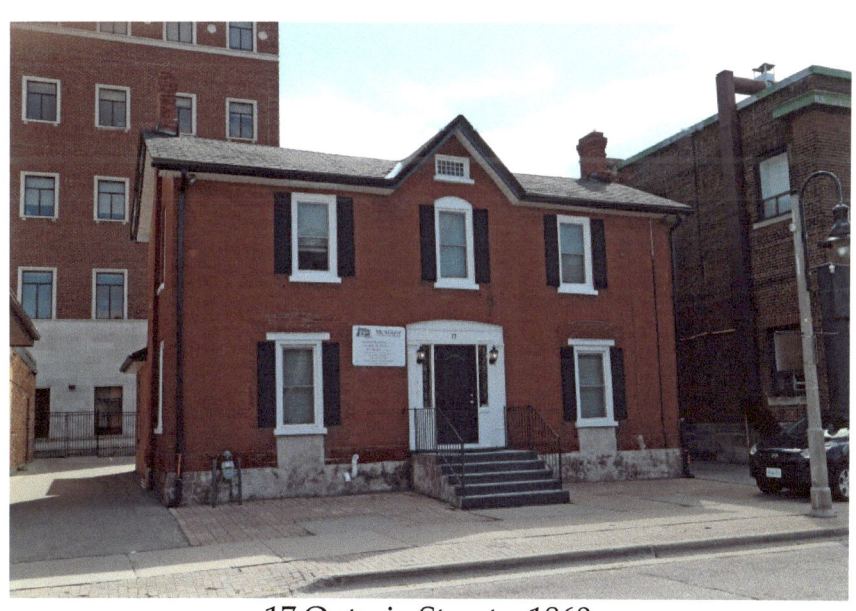

17 Ontario Street – 1860

Building Styles

Edwardian, 1900-1930 – This style bridges the ornate and elaborate styles of the Victorian era and the simplified styles of the 20th century. Edwardian Classicism provided simple, balanced facades, simple rooflines, dormer windows, large front porches, and smooth brick surfaces. Voussoirs and keystones are used sparingly and are understated. Finials and cresting are absent. Cornice brackets and braces are block-like and openings have flat arches or plain stone lintels.

Georgian, before 1860 – This style began with the British King Georges in the 18th century. These buildings have balanced facades around a central door, medium-pitched gable roofs, and small paned windows.

Gothic Revival, 1830-1890 – These decorative buildings have sharply-pitched gables with highly detailed verge boards, pointed-arch window openings, and dichromatic brickwork. It is a common style in Ontario.

Neo-Gothic (Collegiate Gothic): is monochromatic and on a much grander scale than Gothic. Early Neo-Gothic was the decorative use of Gothic elements with a lack of knowledge and understanding of Gothic construction. Neo-Gothic tried to understand the basic principles of Gothic and used them. Early neo-Gothic churches were often plastered or painted, later neo-Gothic churches were not. An important moment in the development of Neo-Gothic is the year 1853, when the hierarchy of the Roman Catholic church was fully restored in the Netherlands. Materials used were natural stone combined with brick. Around the year 1850 Neo-Gothicism was maturing and increasingly became a Roman Catholic style almost exclusively. Neo-Gothic was adopted as the style for schools and universities in the early years of the 20th century. The style became so common for scholastic buildings that it is often called Collegiate Gothic. Wall buttresses and finials are added, but they are generally far too small to be of any structural benefit.

Other Books by Barbara Raue

Coins of Gold
Arrows, Indians and Love
The Life and Times of Barbara
The Cromwell Family Book
Laura Secord Discovered
Daddy Where Are You?

Montana Series
Book 1: Montana Dream
Book 2: Life on the Montana Frontier
Book 3: Montana to Boston and Back
Book 4: Montana Sons Go to War
Book 5: Montana Sons Return from War

Donaldson Series
Book 1: Rite of Passage
Book 2: Rite of Marriage

© 2021 by Barbara Raue - All the photos in this book have been taken with my cameras. I own the rights to them.

Barbara is The Authority on Saving Our History One Photo at a Time. She is pursuing her interest in photography and architecture by preserving a record through photos of old buildings from the 1800s and 1900s with their unique architecture. Enjoy the beautiful architecture in the comfort of your living room. Dream about what it was like in those by-gone days. Dream about what it was like to live in a mansion like one of those in this book.

Barbara Raue, a wife, mother and grandmother, is an avid reader and writer. She has researched and compiled several family histories. In 2010, Barbara published her book "Coins of Gold," which celebrates the courageous life of her mother, May Todd. Barbara's second book is a historical fiction "Arrows, Indians and Love" which takes place in Boonesborough, Kentucky during the time of Daniel Boone. In 2013, Barbara published *The Cromwell Family Book* in which she traces her ancestry generations back into Great Britain. Her second novel is called *Laura Secord Discovered,* in which the story of Laura's service during the War of 1812 is shared. Barbara's memoir is titled *Daddy Where Are You?* It tells of her life growing up without a father. Five novels in the Montana Series have been published, *Montana Dream, Life on the Montana Frontier, Montana to Boston and Back, Montana Sons Go to War,* and *Montana Sons Return from War*. The Donaldson series of two novels is available: *Rite of Passage* and *Rite of Marriage*.

This is a link to Barbara's website to view all of her books
http://barbararaue.ca

www.ingramcontent.com/pod-product-compliance
Lightning Source LLC
Chambersburg PA
CBHW040239220526
45473CB00001B/304